AN OUTLINE OF GREAT WESTERN LOCOMOTIVE
PRACTICE, 1837-1947

An Outline of

GREAT WESTERN LOCOMOTIVE PRACTICE
1837 — 1947

H. HOLCROFT

LONDON

IAN ALLAN

First published 1957
This edition 1971
Second impression 1972

SBN 7110 0228 2

*Printed in Great Britain
by Unwin Brothers Limited
The Gresham Press, Old Woking, Surrey, England
A member of the Staples Printing Group*

Contents

•

Unless otherwise credited, all photographs reproduced in this book are by the Locomotive Publishing Company. The bracketed numbers at the end of each caption refer to the page on which the locomotive is described.

Foreword

by

SIR WILLIAM A. STANIER, D.SC., F.R.S., HON. M.I.MECH.E., M.I.LOCO.E ,
formerly Chief Mechanical Engineer of the London, Midland & Scottish Railway Company

As an old Great Western man, it has given me a great deal of pleasure to read " An Outline of Great Western Locomotive Practice " by Mr. H. Holcroft.

It refers to many incidents with which I am familiar, and which I have been very familiar with from my earliest youth as, like Mr. Holcroft, my father started at Stafford Road, Wolverhampton, and worked under and with many people to whom he refers.

This book should become an historical document, as it covers a very long and important period of Great Western history.

W. A. STANIER.

Preface

The Great Western was the only English railway to preserve its identity from the time of incorporation to the day of unification, when all railways in the United Kingdom were taken over by the State and styled British Railways. The company never experienced the upheavals arising from amalgamation. Such railways as it absorbed over the years were relatively small, and this applied in particular to the Grouping of 1923, when all existing railways were finally allocated to one of four systems.

Continuity combined with a slow evolution therefore marked its progress, and this applied amongst other activities to the company's locomotive practices. Its succession of Locomotive Engineers were men trained in the service of the company and they carried on its traditions, so that development of practices kept in step with the times rather than with any idiosyncrasy which a newcomer might exhibit.

During 110 years much has been written about the locomotives of the Great Western, their design, construction, operation, maintenance and performance, but these contributions are fragmentary in relation to the whole, and a general survey covering all these phases is less common. It is therefore my aim in this work to give an overall picture of the progress over the years as it appears to me.

The Great Western was at first wholly a broad-gauge railway, which expanded westwards through South Wales and northwards as far as Wolverhampton. Although it acquired standard-gauge railways to the north of Wolverhampton in 1854, the Great Western was not permitted to extend the broad gauge over them. On the contrary, the standard gauge spread southwards by means of mixed-gauge track, until it reached London in 1861, but it was not until 1872 that it was extended to Swindon. During this middle period of Great Western history, Wolverhampton was the principal standard-gauge locomotive works and the largest and most important running centre. By 1875 most of the G.W.R. broad-gauge lines had been converted to standard gauge and Swindon Works was adapted for it under the influence of men who brought their practices from Wolverhampton.

This point has not been sufficiently emphasized by writers covering the development of Swindon. As I was born in Wolverhampton and the social circle in which I was brought up included many Great Western men from the Mechanical and Civil Engineering sides, it was quite in keeping with things that my apprenticeship should have been served at the Stafford Road Works in my home town; here I came to learn a side of G.W.R. history of which less is known or appreciated. My subsequent move to Swindon enabled me to follow in the footsteps of many others mentioned in this survey, and to see matters much as they saw them.

As regards the locomotive engineers whose work is dealt with in the following chapters, George Armstrong was a close friend of my grandfather and the patron of my early days on the Great Western. At Swindon I participated in the design of the standard locomotive under G. J. Churchward, and in the chapter relating to it I have interpolated some personal experiences gained under him; during this time I came to know C. B. Collett, first as Assistant Locomotive Works Manager and later as Manager, whilst F. W. Hawksworth was a contemporary of mine in the drawing office.

My subsequent association with R. E. L. Maunsell's standard locomotives, first on the South Eastern & Chatham Railway and continued after its fusion into the Southern Railway group, ran in parallel to the Collett régime at Swindon, thus affording a basis of comparison and it was a means of seeing the Great Western in better perspective and more impartially than if I had remained with that company.

It is with this background of experiences and associations that I have taken up my pen to make this general survey of Great Western locomotive practice. Through the courtesy of Mr. R. A. Smeddle, Chief Mechanical and Electrical Engineer, Western Region of British Railways, the manuscript of this book has been carefully vetted by reference to the official records at Swindon. Sir William Stanier, who is mentioned in a number of places, has also read through the manuscript and has been good enough to signify his approval by contributing a Foreword to this work.

The close scrutiny that has been given therefore confers upon this book a degree of authenticity with which it might not otherwise be credited.

H.H.

Chapter One

In The Days of Daniel Gooch

THE line from London to Bristol was originally built to Brunel's grandiose 7 ft. gauge. It traversed a purely agricultural country, and beyond the county town of Reading there was then no large centre of population en route. The attempt to carry the line through the more industrialised part of the West Country was strongly opposed, as this region was traversed by the Great West Road and the Thames & Avon Canal, and a third means of transport was held to be superfluous.

For this reason a more northerly détour had to be made and the line was carried through the Vale of White Horse, reaching the summit level at Swindon, then but a small market town. From this point the trend was downhill, through Chippenham, but beyond here the level of the River Avon could only be reached by driving the Box Tunnel, two miles long on a falling gradient of 1 in 100. The river was followed by easy gradients through Bath to the terminus at Bristol. The section from London to Didcot was on a ruling gradient of 1 in 1,320 up and no curve was of less than two miles radius. Although from Didcot to Swindon the gradient stiffened to about 1 in 800, it was a comparatively easy ascent, with but short stretches of 1 in 660 up.

From this it is clear that the locomotive working called for east of Swindon was less exacting then on the section west of that point, which involved the steep climb through Box Tunnel and up Dauntsey Bank, about $1\frac{1}{2}$ miles of 1 in 100. As far as the nature of the traffic was concerned, this was mainly through passenger and freight between London and Bristol, and some local passenger and freight services, for much material in bulk still travelled by canal and the lighter loads by road.

Construction of the railway, which took several years, commenced at the London end in 1837 and the line was opened to traffic section by section as work progressed. Although the gauge adopted in the first instance was given as 7 ft. 0 in., the exact dimension to which the rails were laid was 7 ft. 0$\frac{1}{4}$ in. No experience had as yet been gained as to the amount of flange clearance needed on the wider gauge, and it is possible that the wheels of the rolling stock ordered by Brunel were found on arrival to require a little more freedom and that the additional $\frac{1}{4}$ in. was adopted for this purpose. In fact, the first section of the line from Paddington as far as Maidenhead was largely experimental, and modifications had to be made before it was satisfactory and further extension resumed.

In order to obtain locomotive power to operate the traffic, Brunel invited various locomotive builders to supply what they considered to be suitable designs, provided they observed some stipulations which he laid down. Great civil engineer though he was, Brunel's association with locomotives was limited and he was very much in the hands of the builders.   The collection of engines which he secured was berthed in a roundhouse at Bishops Road, Paddington, and to operate and maintain them he appointed as Locomotive Superintendent, Daniel Gooch, a product of the Stephenson school of locomotive engineering round Newcastle and then but 21 years of age. Gooch in turn sent for Archibald Sturrock, with whom he had been associated at Dundee, to become his Assistant.

Most of the early locomotive stock was miscellaneous in character, unsatisfactory in performance and unreliable in service and so the directors, going over Brunel's head, instructed Gooch to prepare his own design and obtain a further batch of engines from locomotive builders.   Valuable experience had been gained in this struggle to keep things going, the good points and the bad were noted, and so the design was largely based on the most efficient and reliable of the locomotives, namely the Stephenson-built *North Star* (Fig. 1).

Like the majority of locomotives then in service, the new design was a 2-2-2 type tender engine, the main frames being outside the wheels and of the slotted sandwich pattern compounded of wooden slabs and thin iron plates bolted together.   Inside stay plates carried additional bearings for the driving wheels, which were 7 ft. in diameter and driven by cylinders 15 in. diameter by 18 in. stroke.   The boiler had a firebox casing of the haycock type to give additional steam space.   The total heating surface was 699 sq. ft. and the grate area 13.5 sq. ft., a working pressure of 50 lb. per sq. in. being adopted.   The four-wheeled tender had slotted sandwich frames and laminated bearing springs located above the frames.   The laminated springs on the locomotive were neatly tucked away between the flitch plates of the outside frame.   Orders for a total of 62 engines of the " Firefly " class (Fig. 2) were placed with seven engine-building firms, and in order to effect complete interchangeability of parts, specifications were drawn up, drawings and templates supplied and rigid compliance with them was insisted upon. This is believed to be the first occasion on which such a plan was put into force.

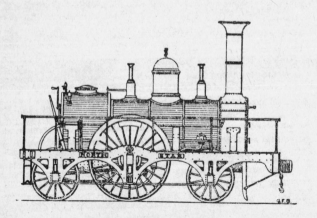

Fig. 1

North Star

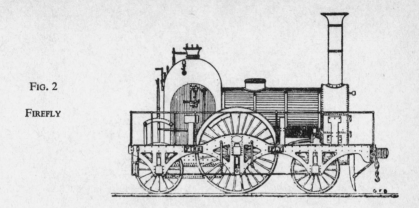

FIG. 2

FIREFLY

With the line to Bristol nearing completion, the question of providing a central depot at which locomotives could be repaired and constructed had to be considered, and with this object in view Brunel and Gooch visited Swindon in the summer of 1840. At the foot of the hill on which the old market town stood and about a mile distant from it, the Cheltenham & Great Western Union Railway joined the main line and a running shed and works was visualised on level ground in the fork between the two lines. Swindon was the summit of the railway, equally accessible to Bristol and London and a convenient place for changing engines; those with 7 ft. diameter wheels were to be used for London trains and others with 6 ft. wheels for the harder Bristol section. The Wilts & Berks Canal could bring in coal, coke and other materials in bulk, through its connections, but a new community would have to be housed if enginemen, fitters, labourers and works staff were to be stationed here. The Directors authorised the plan and a start was soon made on the running shed, workshops and the beginnings of the town of New Swindon, as it was named.

The line to Bristol was opened throughout in 1841, but further extensions were in hand as the G.W.R. was to provide locomotive power for the Bristol & Exeter Railway for its first five years. It was also agreed that the G.W.R. should furnish the locomotives for the Cheltenham line. For working west of Swindon, Gooch designed the " Sun " class (Fig. 3), a smaller edition of his " Firefly " class with 6 ft. diameter wheels. A total of 21 engines was built by three firms. *Hesperus* of this class had Hadotham's return-tube boiler fitted.

Following on these, Gooch designed some 2-4-0 type tender engines for dealing with freight traffic (Fig. 4). They had 5 ft. diameter wheels and sandwich frames outside the wheels, outside cranks being provided for the coupling rods. The boiler had a firebox casing of the haycock type. Three firms supplied a total of 18 engines to this design in the period 1841-42.

For heavier freight duties Gooch designed an 0-6-0 type tender engine (Fig. 5), and four were built by a contractor. They had 5 ft. diameter

FIG. 3

HESPERUS

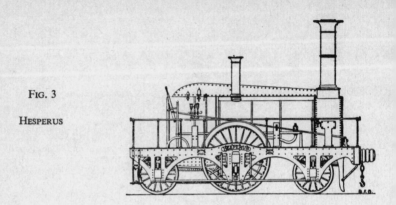

FIG. 4

LEO

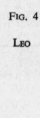

FIG. 5

TITYOS

wheels, 15 in. by 18 in. cylinders and a boiler of similar dimensions to the
" Firefly " class of single-wheelers. The sandwich frames were outside the
wheels and outside cranks provided for the coupling rods, as in the case of
the 2-4-0 type engine.

A pause of several years now occurred before the building of further
engines, but in the interval the G.W.R. broad-gauge mileage was expanding
by the construction of branch lines and other companies were constructing
lines to the wider gauge. This growth brought to a head the gauge contro-
versy, and Brunel had hard work to defend his choice of 7 ft. against the
advocates of the 4 ft. 8½ in. gauge originating with the Stephensons. The
general opinion expressed, however, was that 7 ft. was too wide and 4 ft.
8½ in. too narrow and that a 5 ft. 3 in. or 5 ft. 6 in. gauge would be ideal.
Profiting by this view railways built later on in Ireland, Spain, Russia, India
and Australia all exceeded by some inches the 4 ft. 8½ in. generally adopted
in England, Europe and America.

The Government set up a Gauge Commission to go into the matter and
locomotive trials were held on the rival gauges. The performance set up
by an engine of the " Firefly " class far exceeded anything the narrow-gauge
rivals could put up, but notwithstanding this, the Commission, in view of
the large mileage of 4 ft. 8½ in. track already existing, recommended that it
should be regarded as the standard gauge to which future railways should be
constructed, so that the 7 ft. gauge was looked upon as an outsize.

To strengthen their case, the G.W.R. directors instructed Gooch to
produce an engine of greater power than his " Firefly " class, and the resulting
design was an enlarged edition of that class, having 8 ft. diameter driving
wheels, 18 in. by 24 in. cylinders, 1,733 sq. ft. of heating surface, a grate
area of 22.6 sq. ft. and a boiler pressure of 100 lb. per sq. in. It was provided
with a six-wheeled tender.

Swindon Works was by this time sufficiently complete to undertake the
construction of Gooch's designs, and Archibald Sturrock, who had been
moved there from Paddington, was Assistant Locomotive Superintendent
and Works Manager. Sturrock turned out the famous engine *Great Western*
(Fig. 6) in April, 1846, and its performance on the road in speed and hauling
power was far in excess of any locomotive so far extant.

While experience was being gained with this prototype, six more tender
engines of the 2-2-2 type were turned out from Swindon in 1846-47, namely
the " Prince " class (Fig. 7). They had 16 in. by 24 in. cylinders, 7 ft. wheels,
a heating surface of 982 sq. ft. and a grate area of 13.6 sq. ft. The boiler
had the usual haycock firebox casing, but the sandwich frames were behind
the wheels, instead of outside as heretofore. These smaller engines were
intended for use on the new branch lines which were being opened.

A fracture of *Great Western's* leading axle, due, it was thought, to excessive axle loading, brought the engine back to shops. The frames were
lengthened to take two pairs of leading wheels, one inverted laminated spring
on each side of the engine being provided for two axleboxes, so that it also
served as an equaliser to ensure proper distribution of weight between the
wheels. By this addition the rigid wheelbase was increased from 16 ft. to
18 ft. 11½ in., conducing to steadier running at speed and avoiding any

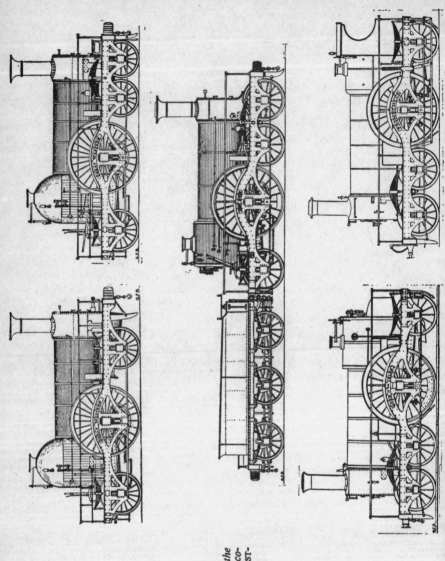

Fig. 6

The development of the broad-gauge express locomotive from Great Western to Prometheus

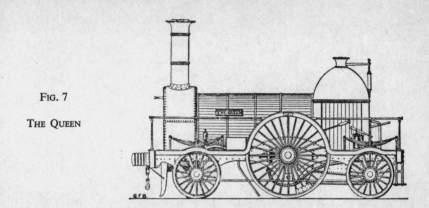

FIG. 7

THE QUEEN

tendency to crab-wise movement. Although 16 ft. might be more than ample for the standard gauge, however, it was comparatively short in relation to the broad gauge.

With this alteration the first phase was ended. Design had been consistant in that all engines had well marked features in common. From 1847 onwards a second, and final, phase commenced which lasted to the end of the days of the broad gauge. Again design was consistent and characteristic once the change had been made.

With the appearance of the " Iron Duke " class, an improved version of the *Great Western*, many new features were adopted. The boiler had a raised round top firebox casing and a mid-feather was provided inside the firebox. The safety valves situated over the firebox casing had a neat cylindrical cover of polished brass with a rim at the top and a square base. Sheet iron plates covered the wood lagging and these were encircled by polished brass bands. Owing to the width of the firebox back, a pull-out lever was arranged for the grid-type regulator on the front of the smokebox tubeplate and brought control within easy reach of the driver. The inside

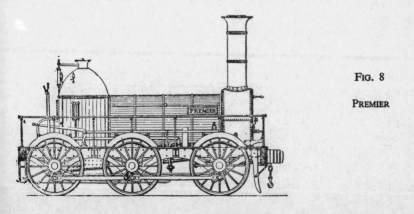

FIG. 8

PREMIER

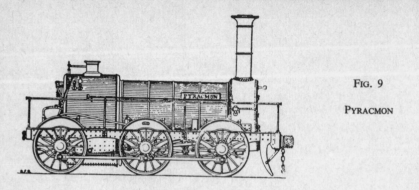

Fig. 9

Pyracmon

frame was more fully developed and an additional stay carried a fifth, and centre, bearing for the crank axle. The Gooch valve gear replaced the old gab motion. In all, 29 of the " Iron Duke " class were built, six in 1847, 12 in the period 1848-50, four in 1850-51 and finally a locomotive building firm supplied seven in 1854-55.

The first engine to be built at Swindon was one of the " Premier " 0-6-0 type goods engines (Fig. 8) with 16 in by 24 in. cylinders and 5 ft. diameter wheels. They appeared in 1846-47 and were the last to have the haycock firebox casing, but the most important feature about them was that the sandwich frames were situated behind the wheels, so that outside cranks were not needed and the coupling rods were attached to crank pins in the wheel bosses. Six more 0-6-0 engines, the " Pyracmon " class (Fig. 9) of 1847-48, had boilers with the raised round top firebox casing, and they were followed by eight more, the " Caesar " class of 1851-52.

The first tank engines were two saddletanks of the 4-4-0 type for passenger working (Fig. 10), which were turned out from Swindon in 1849. They had 17 in. by 24 in. cylinders and 6 ft. wheels. The sandwich frames were behind the drivers, but did not extend forward of them on account of the bogie, which was carried on a centre pin attached to a bracket fastened

Fig. 10

Corsair

[*H. Gordon Tidey*

A down fast train in Twyford cutting headed by "Saint" Class 4-6-0 No. 2980 *Coeur de Lion*, rebuild of a 2-cylinder Atlantic design of 1905.

Armstrong Standard Goods No. 31 (as reboilered and with addition of cab). (25)

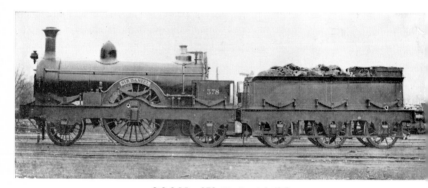

2-2-2 No. 378 *Sir Daniel*. (26)

2-2-2 No. 55 *Queen*. (27)

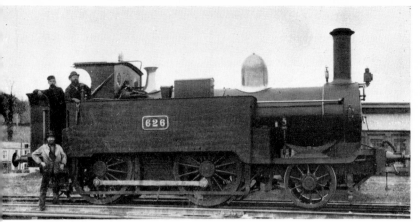

Armstrong's 2-4-0T No. 626 (as re-boilered and with addition of cab). (27)

Armstrong's 0-6-0 Saddle Tank No. 1279 (with later full length tank). (27)

Armstrong's 2-4-0T No. 974 with outside bearings to leading wheels. (27)

11

2-2-2 No. 999 *Sir Alexander*. (27)

G, Armstrong's 0-4-2 Saddle Tank No. 517. (34)

" 517 " class engine No. 521 rebuilt with side tanks (34)

FIG. 11

CATO

to the underside of the front end of the boiler barrel. Another batch of 13 supplied by contractors in 1854-55 differed in having 5 ft. 9 in. wheels. The saddle tank, which covered the boiler barrel only, carried 900 gal. of water.

Thereafter some of the early engines obtained by Brunel were rebuilt as saddletanks for use on branch lines, and the greater adhesive weight resulting enabled more use to be made of them. Saddletanks were much used on the broad-gauge line in preference to side tanks. The raising of the centre of gravity was of no consequence on the wider gauge, and the tanks were easily removed; moreover, when in place they caused the minimum of obstruction to the carrying out of boiler repairs. The locomotives of the South Devon Railway were practically all saddletanks, whether for passenger or goods working.

The Bristol & Exeter Railway had acquired its own locomotive stock by 1849, and so returned those on loan from the G.W.R. On the other hand, the failure of the atmospheric system with which the South Devon Railway had been equipped on Brunel's recommendation led to its abandonment and the hiring of locomotives from the G.W.R. The opening of the South Wales

FIG. 12

PLATO

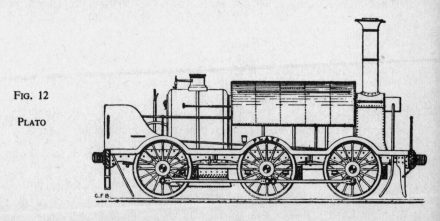

Railway from Gloucester to Milford in 1850 and its operation by the G.W.R. required the provision of more locomotives, and this was followed two years later by the opening of the northern extension of the broad gauge from Didcot as far as Birmingham.

These extensions called for more motive power. To meet the demand, Gooch designed his standard 0-6-0 type goods engine (Fig. 11), of which no fewer than 102 were built at Swindon over the period 1852-63, 22 of them during 1852-54. They were similar in design to the " Caesar " class, but had 17 in. by 24 in. cylinders, a heating surface of 1,574 sq. ft. and a grate area of 19.2 sq. ft., boiler pressure being raised to 120 lb. per sq. in.

Besides making their own extensions, the G.W.R. gave powerful backing to Bills presented to Parliament for the building of other companies' broad-gauge lines. In 1844 they had reached Oxford from Didcot, and the Oxford, Worcester & Wolverhampton Railway was granted powers to build a line in mixed gauge onwards. Brunel's estimate for the cost of building of the line soon proved quite inadequate, and the company was involved in financial difficulties. The G.W.R. refused to help, so the O.W. & W.R. laid in only the standard-gauge rails of the projected mixed gauge, and the G.W.R. got no further north here. They were, however, constructing a line to Rugby from Oxford, while broad-gauge companies, the Birmingham & Oxford Junction Railway and the Birmingham, Wolverhampton & Dudley Railway were authorised. The G.W.R. took over these companies and built the lines projected, with the net result that the line to Rugby reached no further than Fenny Compton, where it met the B. & O.J.R. Instead, the broad gauge was pushed northwards to Snow Hill, Birmingham, and the service of trains was inaugurated in 1852 by a train drawn by the famous 8 ft. single-wheeler *Lord of the Isles*, newly dismounted from its stand at the Great Exhibition of 1851 in Hyde Park, London.

Still pressing onwards to carry the broad gauge north to the Mersey, the G.W.R. was negotiating for control of the Shrewsbury & Birmingham Railway and the Shrewsbury & Chester Railway during the time they were constructing the line from Birmingham to Wolverhampton. Actually it joined the Oxford, Worcester & Wolverhampton Railway at Priestfield Junction, and mixed gauge carried trains of both railways to a joint station in Wolverhampton. The G.W.R.'s bid to take over the two Shrewsbury railways was strenuously opposed by their rival, the London & North Western Railway, and although the G.W.R. ultimately won their case it was with the proviso that the broad gauge should not be carried north of Wolverhampton. Thus they had to rest content with standard-gauge feeders to their northern outpost, and so for the first time the G.W.R. possessed standard-gauge rolling stock.

The broad gauge to Wolverhampton was completed in 1854, and an extention to Oxley Viaduct in mixed gauge enabled the Shrewsbury & Birmingham trains to be diverted to the joint station with the O.W. & W.R., instead of continuing to the L. & N.W.R. station in Wolverhampton, as formerly. Mixed gauge was laid also from Oxley Viaduct over the S. & B.R. line into the town, so that broad-gauge goods trains could be dealt with there at Victoria Basin, a canal transhipment point.

Although separate companies, the two Shrewsbury lines had been operated by a joint committee and had established a running shed and works for the repair of their rolling stock at a point on the Stafford Road in Wolverhampton. Joseph Armstrong had charge of the running and repairs here, and he and his establishment were taken over by the G.W.R. A broad-gauge running shed was then built on the opposite side of the Stafford Road to the works, being reached by a short branch off the northern extension at Cannock Road Junction. Armstrong was also given charge of the running north of Oxford, so forming the Northern Division of the G.W.R.

The directors decided that they would construct all their standard-gauge locomotives at the Stafford Road Works, independently of Swindon, there being no rail connection to do otherwise. The works had been planned solely on a maintenance basis and with no provision for new construction. Before locomotives could be built, additional shops, a forge, foundry and boiler shop would have to be laid down and equipped, but there was no room for this as yet. A new goods station and yard had first to be constructed in the centre of Wolverhampton to which the activities of the goods station and yard of the former S. & B.R. at Stafford Road could be transferred and a new running shed had to be built near Stafford Road Junction, adjacent to Oxley Viaduct, to give space for an erecting shop, and the carriage and wagon work was transferred to the original S. & C.R. Works at Saltney, near Chester.

The locomotive stock of 56 engines taken over from the two Shrewsbury lines was very miscellaneous, and the amalgamation with the G.W.R. brought about increased traffic. As the building of new locomotives at Stafford Road could not begin for some years it was decided that Daniel Gooch should supply a nucleus of new engines of sound design to supplement the existing stock, after which Armstrong would build his own when the shops were in a position to do so.

The present Paddington station was completed in 1854 and the company's offices were established there, whereupon Gooch moved into them from his quarters at Westbourne Park shed, which had superseded the roundhouse at Bishops Road. After this came the first design for the standard gauge, a goods engine of the 0-6-0 type with 15½ in. by 22 in. cylinders and 5 ft. wheels (Fig. 12). It had all the characteristics of his broad-gauge engines as

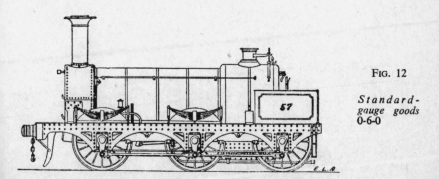

Fig. 12

Standard-gauge goods 0-6-0

FIG. 13

No. 69, 2-2-2 passenger locomotive, standard gauge

regards motion, boiler and framing, but on account of the narrower width the sandwich frames were outside the wheels and outside cranks had to be used for the coupling rods.   Twelve engines, Nos. 57 to 68, were constructed to this design at Swindon in 1855-56, and they had to be conveyed to Wolverhampton over the broad gauge in specially-constructed well wagons.   It was said that this job was not at all to the liking of Swindon, who regarded it as an indignity to have to produce other than broad-gauge locomotives. They were the aristocrats!

Simultaneously with the goods engine, Gooch produced the design for a 2-2-2 type passenger engine with 6 ft. 6 in. wheels (Fig. 13).   Not only did it have all the characteristics of the broad gauge, but boiler, cylinders, motion and other parts were common and interchangeable with the goods engine. Eight to this design, Nos. 69 to 76, were built by Beyers, Manchester, then newly established, and they were the first engines to be turned out by that firm.   Interchangeability of parts between engines of a class, initiated in Gooch's " Firefly" class of 1840, was now extended to such interchangeability between engines of more than one class, and the beginnings of standardisation were afoot.

Two goods engines of the 0-6-0 type left on Beyer's hands, presumably by a cancelled order, were taken over by the G.W.R.   They were inside

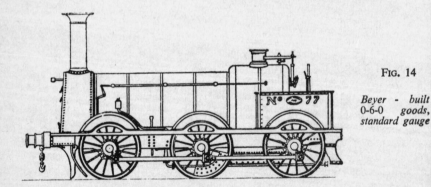

FIG. 14

Beyer - built 0-6-0 goods, standard gauge

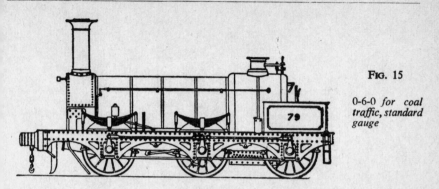

FIG. 15

0-6-0 *for coal traffic, standard gauge*

framed with Stephenson link motion, 5 ft. wheels and 16 in. by 24 in. cylinders. These, Nos. 77 and 78, were, however, furnished with the Gooch design of boiler before delivery (Fig. 14). For heavy coal traffic in North Wales, Gooch modified his goods engine design to produce mineral engines with 4 ft. 6 in. wheels and 16 in. by 24 in. cylinders (Fig. 15). Twelve were built at Swindon in 1857, Nos. 79 to 90. Here again was standardisation of parts.

Four saddle-tank engines for the broad gauge were constructed at Swindon in 1852-54. They had the same dimensions as the standard goods engines, but carried saddletanks of about 750 gal. capacity over the boiler barrel (see Fig. 11). In 1855 R. Stephenson & Co. supplied 10 handsome broad-gauge engines of the 4-4-0 type, the "Waverley" class (Fig. 16). They had 7 ft. wheels and 17 in. by 24 in. cylinders; heating surface was 1,574 sq. ft. and grate area 19.2 sq. ft. As in the "Iron Duke" single wheelers there were two pairs of leading wheels, but being coupled engines, the sandwich frames were placed behind all wheels. In other respects the engines had all the characteristics of the Gooch design. They were intended for the South Wales passenger traffic, but for such routes as the Weymouth line, opened in 1857, a lighter design was preferred and the "Victoria" class 2-4-0 type

FIG. 16

LALLA ROOKH, *broad gauge passenger 4-4-0*

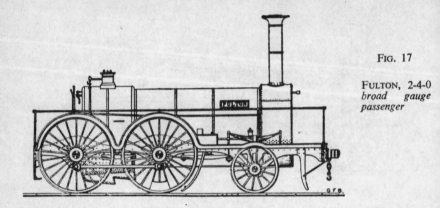

appeared in 1856 (Fig. 17).   Eight were built at Swindon and a further batch
of ten came from there in 1863-64.   They had 6 ft. 6 in. wheels, cylinders
16 in. by 24 in. and boilers with 1,264 sq. ft. heating surface and 13.5 sq. ft.
grate area.

The first portion of the Metropolitan Railway was constructed in shallow
tunnels under London streets from Bishops Road, Paddington, to Farringdon
Street in the City, in 1863.   It was laid in mixed gauge and at first worked
by broad-gauge G.W.R. stock.   A special type of locomotive was called for,
and Gooch provided a 2-4-0 type tank engine with 6 ft. wheels and tanks
below the boiler barrel and footplate.   The 16 in. by 24 in. cylinders had
therefore to be outside and steeply inclined to clear the leading wheels.
Very few of the Gooch features were in evidence; they were the first engines
to have condensing gear for tunnel working, and they had plate frames
(Fig. 18).

The G.W.R. soon fell out with the Metropolitan Railway and withdrew
the broad-gauge stock at short notice.   After borrowing some standard-
gauge stock from the Great Northern Railway as a temporary measure, the
Metropolitan acquired their own stock to standard gauge.   Meanwhile, the
G.W.R. found use for the 22 engines of the class in branch line and local
services after the condensing gear had been removed.   Of these engines, 12
had been built by outside firms in 1862 and 10 at Swindon in 1863-64.

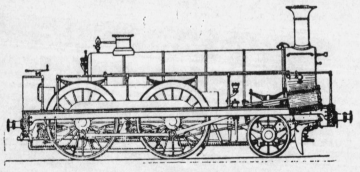

In the Northern Division the standard-gauge working flourished while that of the broad gauge withered.   Althouth Wolverhampton station had been fully laid out for change-of-gauge transfer of passengers, mail and parcels traffic, it was found more convenient to run the Chester trains to Birmingham over mixed gauge and make the change there.   The mixed-gauge working was extended southwàrds, first to Oxford, then to Didcot, Reading and Basingstoke, and finally to Paddington in 1861.   Provision had to be made at Westbourne Park shed for the accommodation of standard gauge engines and a large extension of the running sheds at Wolverhampton was carried out.

In the previous year the G.W.R. had taken over the Birkenhead Railway jointly with the L. & N.W.R. and so had achieved their goal in reaching the Mersey, though not by broad gauge.   Through trains from Paddington to Birkenhead began running in 1861, and the use of the broad gauge on the Northern Division was limited, being retained for such work as the running of through goods trains from the West of England.   With the standard gauge carried to London, coal trains began running there from Pontypool Road via Hereford, Worcester, Oxford and Didcot and the off-loading of

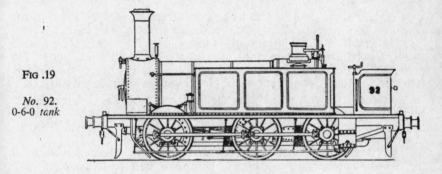

FIG .19

No. 92.
0-6-0 *tank*

new standard-gauge locomotives from Swindon was done at Didcot instead of at Wolverhampton.

This continuous growth of the standard-gauge mileage and the displacement of broad-gauge services called for more new locomotive construction, but the Stafford Road Works were overwhelmed with the increasing number of engines which they had to maintain and so could not get going with new work in any quantity.   Swindon had, accordingly, to continue to provide further assistance, and two 0-6-0 type tank engines, Nos. 91 and 92 (Fig. 19), were supplied in 1860.   These had 4 ft. 2 in. wheels and 15 in. by 22 in. cylinders, but departures from the usual Gooch design occurred in the provision of side tanks and adoption of inside plate frames.   Another twelve engines for mineral traffic, as previously supplied, Nos. 119 to 130, followed in 1861-62.

To cope with the situation, the shops at Wolverhampton had to be duplicated by the erection of new buildings on the broad-gauge side of Stafford Road, and until these could become effective new locomotives had to be supplied from elsewhere.   Eighteen more goods engines were built in

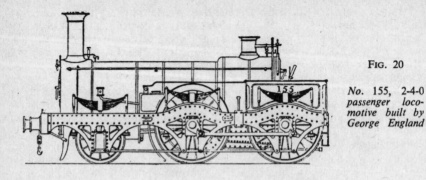

FIG. 20

No. 155, 2-4-0 passenger locomotive built by George England

1862, six by Swindon and twelve by the Avonside Works, Bristol, but a significant change was the substitution of the Stephenson link motion for that of Gooch. The latter has a constant lead whereas the lead of the Stephenson gear is variable and so results in a livelier performance, and it would seem that Armstrong prevailed upon Gooch to agree to the change.

Next to appear were eight 2-4-0 type passenger engines, Nos. 149 to 156 (Fig. 20), which were built by George England & Co., and ten 2-2-2 type, Nos. 157 to 165 (Fig. 21), by Sharp, Stewart & Co. They had all the characteristic Gooch practices except that Stephenson link motion was adopted in both cases. From Swindon came ten more goods engines of the 131-148 series, Nos. 310 to 319, the last of the Gooch design for standard gauge.

In 1863 the G.W.R. took over the West Midland Railway, which had been formed by the amalgamation of the Oxford, Worcester & Wolverhampton and the Newport, Abergavenny & Hereford Railways, and with it a half-share with the L. & N.W.R. of the Shrewsbury & Hereford Railway, which they jointly operated. These acquisitions resulted in a further increase of the varied assortment of locomotives which the Stafford Road Works had to maintain, while the area of country served had grown so large that the Worcester Division had to be formed to relieve the Northern Division of the southern half of it.

At this period the G.W.R. was virtually in two sections, the standard

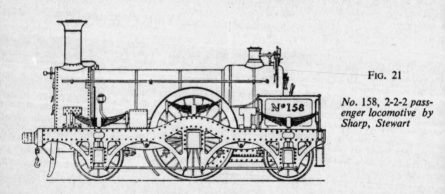

FIG. 21

No. 158, 2-2-2 passenger locomotive by Sharp, Stewart

gauge serving an area bounded to the west by London, Oxford, Worcester, Newport, Shrewsbury, Chester and Birkenhead, with locomotives based on Wolverhampton, and the broad gauge covering points as widely separated as London, Swindon, Weymouth, Bristol, Gloucester, Cardiff and Milford, with locomotives based on Swindon.

To Daniel Gooch, an enthusiastic supporter of Brunel's 7 ft. gauge, this ever-advancing wave of standard-gauge track must have been disheartening. It was becoming generally recognised that the broad gauge was obsolescent and its continued survival only a matter of time, so he therefore resigned to seek adventure anew by the laying of the first Atlantic cable from Brunel's famous steamship, the *Great Eastern.* At a second attempt this was accomplished, and Gooch was made a baronet by Queen Victoria in recognition of his part in this great achievement.

On return, he secured election to Parliament as the Member for the Cricklade Division of Wiltshire, in which Swindon then stood. He was invited to join the Board of Directors and was elected Chairman of the Great Western Railway, a position he held until his death in 1889.

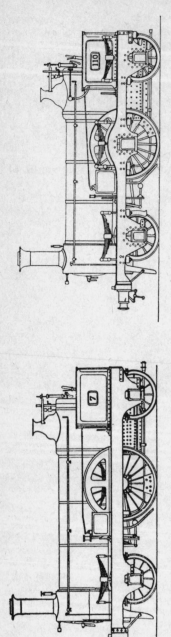

FIG. 23. 2-2-2 No. 110, built in 1862

FIG. 22. The first Armstrong design: 2-2-2 No. 7, built in 1858

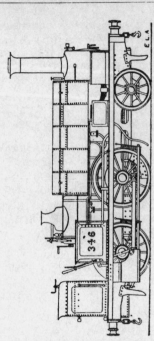

FIG. 25. 2-4-0 saddle tank, built in 1864

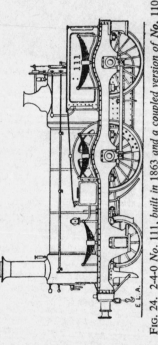

FIG. 24. 2-4-0 No. 111, built in 1863 and a coupled version of No. 110

Chapter Two

THE REVOLUTION UNDER JOSEPH ARMSTRONG

A FTER being taken into the service of the G.W.R. at Wolverhampton in 1854, Joseph Armstrong had to wait four years before he had an opportunity to show his hand in design, owing to the circumstances related in the previous chapter. When two of the Shrewsbury & Chester engines had to be scrapped, he replaced them in 1858 by two single-wheelers of his own design, Nos. 7 and 8, of the 2-2-2 type (Fig. 22). These had inside bearings to the driving wheels in the inside frames, while the leading and trailing wheels had bearings in an outside frame of single plate. This style of framing originated with George Gray of the Hull & Selby Railway, under whom Armstrong had served, and he took the first opportunity to revive it. Gray's design had been developed by David Joy of E. B. Wilson & Co. in the famous " Jenny Lind " class built by that firm.

The boilers of Armstrong's engines were like those of Gooch, domeless and with raised round top firebox casings. Armstrong, however, adopted his own characteristic design of safety valve casing, which could be described as a large diameter base joined to a smaller diameter top portion by an ogee curve. The copper top of the chimney had a rim somewhat smaller in diameter than that favoured by Gooch. All Armstrong's designs included the Stephenson link motion.

Two more of these single-wheelers, Nos. 30 and 32, were built at Wolverhampton in 1860, and in 1862 appeared another of the 2-2-2 type, No. 110 (Fig. 23), but this differed from the previous engines in having bearings for the driving wheels in the outside frame, so that the crank axle had four bearings. The cylinders were 15 in. diameter by 22 in. stroke and the driving wheels were 6 ft. in diameter. This engine is of importance to history in that it was the ancestor from which successive G.W.R. single-wheelers were developed over the years.

In 1863 Stafford Road Works was in a position to take on more new construction, and the first 2-4-0 type appeared (Fig. 24). It was virtually the same as the single-wheeler No. 110, but the trailing carrying wheels were replaced by a pair of coupled wheels and the cylinders were enlarged to 16 in. by 24 in. Six were built, and in 1864 came the first passenger tank engines, three 2-4-0 type saddle tanks with inside frames, 5 ft. diameter wheels and 14 in. by 22 in. cylinders (Fig. 25). In the same year the works built eight 0-6-0 type saddle tanks with double frames, 4 ft. 6 in. wheels and 16 in. by 24 in. cylinders (Fig. 26). These were intended for local goods work and shunting.

With the resignation of Daniel Gooch in 1864, Armstrong was appointed to succeed him and he was also made responsible for the carriage and wagon

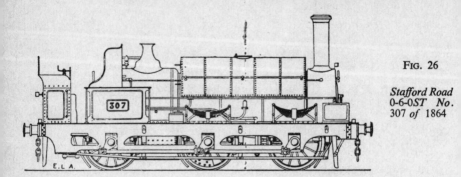

FIG. 26

Stafford Road
0-6-0ST *No.*
307 *of* 1864

stock; thus he became the first Locomotive, Carriage and Wagon Superintendent of the G.W.R., and he set up his headquarters at Swindon and not at Paddington as Gooch had done.   His brother, George Armstrong, took over Stafford Road Works and the Northern Division.

Hitherto the G.W.R. had obtained their carriage and wagon stock from private builders, but about this time it was decided that the company should construct their own stock.   Plans were made for raising the level of land at Cripley Meadow, Oxford, and the erection on it of shops for building and repair of all rolling stock, both broad and standard gauge, there.   The publication of the plan raised a great outcry against the threatened industrialisation of the city; it created a furore in the academical world and was the subject of a cartoon in *Punch*.   Little did these opponents think that some 40 years later one of their own citizens, a cyclemaker by the name of Morris, would inaugurate a far vaster industry within the city's boundaries!

Bowing to the storm, the directors decided to situate the works at Swindon using Saltney Works, Chester, and the old O.W. & W.R. shops at Worcester for standard-gauge vehicles for the time being.   Thus Armstrong was at first preoccupied with the erection of a new works on the south side of the main line at Swindon.

At this time the broad gauge was at its zenith, both as regards track mileage and number of locomotives.   Armstrong had to turn his attention to the provision of further broad-gauge engines, and his first design, known as the " Hawthorn " class (Fig. 27), was a 2-4-0 type tender engine with 6 ft. wheels and 16 in. by 24 in. cylinders.   The boiler had 1,201 sq. ft. of heating surface, a grate area of 19.0 sq. ft. and a pressure of 130 lb. per sq. in.   The " Hawthorn " had plate frames behind the wheels, Stephenson valve gear and the shape of safety valve casing typical of Armstrong.   During 1855-56 a total of 26 engines was built, 20 by the Avonside Engine Company and six by Swindon Works.   Ten of this class were subsequently rebuilt as saddletanks for branch line working.   During the same period Swindon built 14 goods engines of the 0-6-0 type, known as the " Swindon " class. They were similar to Gooch's standard goods but had the Armstrong features which were introduced in the " Hawthorn " class.

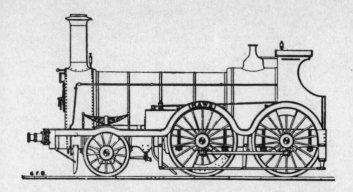

FIG. 27

HAWK,   2-4-0
broad - gauge
tender   loco-
motive

The last broad-gauge locomotives to be built were six side tank engines of the 0-6-0 type, fitted with condensing apparatus for working over the Metropolitan Railway in London.   They were known as the " Sir Watkin" class and were the only side tanks made for the broad gauge.   In addition to the Armstrong features introduced in previous designs, the boilers were provided with domes.

This, in 1866, was the end of the broad-gauge construction, apart from the re-building or complete renewal of Gooch's famous 8 ft. single-wheelers as necessary over the years.   This was carried out to keep the class intact in its original form as a compliment to their creator, who had become Chairman of the company.   As the aristocrats of the railway world, all broad-gauge engines received names befitting their dignity, instead of numbers, which were left to the plebeian standard gauge.

In 1866 came the first of Armstrong's goods engines for the standard gauge (Fig. 28), of which there were twelve, Nos. 360-371.   The outside plate frames were similar to those of his Wolverhampton saddletanks of the " 302" class, in having holes slotted out in the frames so that pieces were left to act as stays between the horns.   The raised top firebox casing of Gooch now disappeared and a dome was added in lieu of the steam space lost at the firebox end.

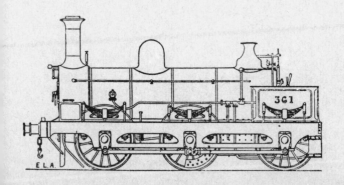

FIG. 28

First Armstrong
0-6-0   standard-
gauge goods

Next to appear was the " Sir Daniel " class of single-wheeler, of which ten were built in 1866, followed by 20 more three years later. They were intended to provide greater power on the Paddington-Wolverhampton services and were an enlargement of No. 110 built at Wolverhampton. They had 17 in. by 24 in. cylinders and 7 ft. driving wheels. The boiler again had a flush top firebox and a dome, but the Armstrong pattern of safety valve casing gave place to Beyer's simpler design, in which a larger diameter base diminished to a smaller diameter top through one curved surface. This polished brass safety valve casing has ever since been a conspicuous feature on G.W.R. locomotives. It first came to the line on two 0-4-0 type saddle-tanks, Nos. 91 and 92, supplied by Beyers in 1857, and later on the 30 goods engines of their design, Nos. 322 to 341 and 350 to 359, in 1864 and 1866 respectively.

Simultaneously with the passenger engines Armstrong produced his standard goods. It was similar to his first goods engine, but the frame tie between horns was dispensed with in favour of a cut-away shape.

Beginning with No. 388, nearly 300 were built over the next ten years. These engines had boilers, cylinders, motion and other details common with the single-wheelers. This applied later on to the mineral engines and to saddle and side tank engines which followed. Armstrong was thus enlarging upon Gooch's policy of standardisation.

About this time the Directors decided that the use of the broad gauge would have to be abandoned in stages, and this meant the entire replacement of the rolling stock by new standard-gauge construction beforehand. Armstrong undertook to do this with the means at his disposal and without going to contractors, given the time.

New construction was now speeded up. To occupy a few pits for new work and to despatch it on wagons over the broad gauge to Didcot, to be set on standard track there, was comparatively easy to accomplish. A far more difficult situation to be faced was the fact that in a few years' time all this stock would be coming to Swindon for general repairs, as Wolverhampton could not cope with more than the locomotives working on the Northern and Worcester Divisions. Swindon Works would have to be adapted to meet the problem when it arose; mixed gauge must be laid throughout and reception sidings prepared to accommodate the quota of broad-gauge stock which would be withdrawn in a single operation at each stage.

To assist him in this task came a number of men from Wolverhampton, including T. White as Chief Clerk; William Dean, Works Manager at Stafford Road, was appointed Armstrong's Principal Assistant, and W. H. Stanier came as Dean's confidential clerk. Swindon Works was now dominated by Wolverhampton men in the key posts, and they carried their methods and practices with them, so that the Swindon of Brunel and Gooch suffered eclipse. For the time being, all the characteristics of the Gooch era—the sandwich frame, the domeless boiler with raised top firebox casing, the Gooch valve motion and other details—disappeared, though in the course of years some came to light again.

In 1868, six 2-4-0 type passenger engines were built, but, unlike Armstrong's earlier " 111 " class, the " 439 " class had inside frames. These engines had 6 ft. 1 in. wheels and 16 in. by 24 in. cylinders. The design was repeated in his subsequent locomotives of the type, the " 481 " class of 1869, the " 717 " class of 1872 and the " 806 " class of 1873, but these later engines had outside bearings for the leading wheels. Twenty side tanks of the 2-4-0 type with 5 ft. coupled wheels built in 1869 had inside bearings to all wheels, and six 0-6-0 type side tanks of 1870 were in line with the standard goods.

The broad-gauge rail from Didcot to Wolverhampton was taken out in 1869 and the material used to extend mixed gauge from Didcot to Swindon, which was reached in 1872. Everything was then ready for the first stage of the conversion, and the Milford to Gloucester and Gloucester to Swindon lines were brought in from 7 ft. to 4 ft. 8½ in. gauge in the course of a few days, after all broad-gauge rolling stock had been evacuated to the reception sidings prepared for them at Swindon. Thereafter standard-gauge trains ran through from Paddington to Milford via Gloucester.

The new construction continued in anticipation of the second stage, and 50 saddle tanks with parts interchangeable with the standard goods were built, together with 20 more of the 2-4-0 type passenger engines, the " 806 " class, which were similar to Armstrong's previous design but had 6 ft. 6½ in. wheels.

In 1873 came the first of his larger single-wheelers, No. 55 *Queen*. It had 7 ft. wheels and 18 in. by 24 in. cylinders. A new departure in this engine was the adoption of two-bar slidebars and a connecting rod with forked end and two-strap type little ends to embrace the crosshead, which was secured to the piston rod by a nut. Hitherto, the four-bar slidebars had been the rule, with single-strap little end and piston rod fastened by cotter. The valve gear had cylindrical guides for the valve rods in place of the usual pendulum links attached to a bracket at the top of the motion plate. It may be that Dean influenced the matter, for he made much use of this type of motion in years following.

In the year 1874 there appeared the 0-6-0 type mineral engine with 4 ft. 6 in. wheels, also some 0-6-0 type saddle tanks. Both of these had parts in common with the standard goods. These mineral engines were much used for the Pontypool Road to Birkenhead via Shrewsbury coal trains. More 2-4-0 type side tanks were built, but, as a result of experience with the 2-4-0 tender engines, these and future batches had outside bearings to the leading wheels.

In 1874, the mixed gauge was laid in to Thingley Junction and Bristol, and at once the second stage of gauge conversion was carried out, including the Weymouth and other lines to the south of the main line. On completion of the work little remained of Brunel's 7 ft. track other than the Paddington to Bristol line and that in mixed gauge. It was back to where it began in 1841! By 1875, standard-gauge rolling stock was used for all traffic except the Paddington-Penzance trains, which had to continue over the broad gauge Bristol & Exeter, South Devon and Cornwall Railways.

The last new design of Armstrong was a single-wheeler with a domeless boiler, the " Sir Alexander " class. Otherwise the 20 engines built were practically duplicates of No. 55 *Queen*. These exceeded the broad-gauge single-wheelers in tractive effort and adhesive weight, though the latter had more boiler power.

A respite for the broad-gauge occurred in 1876, when the Bristol & Exeter, South Devon and Cornwall Railways were taken over by the G.W.R., so that the track mileage was augmented for the time being. On this extension Gooch's 8 ft. single-wheelers ran through as far as Newton Abbot.

The mixed gauge was extended to Exeter, and the B. & E.R. shops at Bristol were closed and repairs transferred to Swindon Works. Pearson's famous 4-2-4 type tank engines with 9 ft. driving wheels were taken in hand and rebuilt as 4-2-2 tender engines with 8 ft. wheels in line with Gooch's single-wheelers, but they differed from them in having the frames behind the wheels and a bogie in place of the two pairs of carrying wheels. Apart from this there was little in the way of rebuilding during the Armstrong era, for the broad-gauge engines were obsolescent and the standard-gauge engines but recently built.

Worn out by his exertions, Armstrong died after a few days' illness in 1877. In the brief space of 13 years he had built the carriage works, rearranged the locomotive shops and constructed all the locomotive and coaching stock that was needed for replacement of the broad-gauge stock. In this he had been aided by his brother George Armstrong, whom he had left in charge at Stafford Road, and who supervised addition of a substantial number of new locomotives from the Wolverhampton Works.

Joseph Armstrong's Principal Assistant, William Dean, was duly appointed to succeed him.

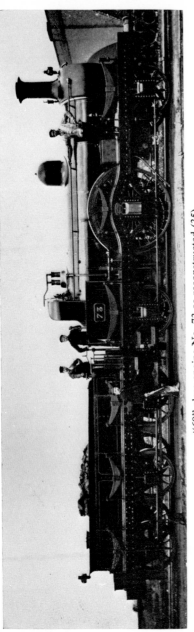

"69" class engine No. 73 as reconstructed (35).

"57" class engine No. 64 as reconstructed (35).

No. 633 as rebuilt with condensing apparatus. (36)

" 645 " Class 0-6-0 Saddle Tank No. 651. (36)

" 850 " Class shunting tank No. 990. (36)

30

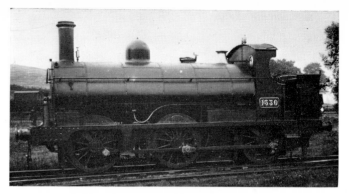

" 1501 " class Saddle Tank No. 1530. (36)

" 1216 " class shunting tank No. 1227. (36)

" 79 " class mineral engine No. 84 as reconstructed. (36)

31

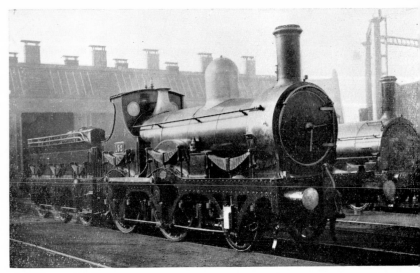

" 149 " class 2-4-0 passenger engine No. 152 as reconstructed. (37)

" 439 " class 2-4-0 passenger engine No. 444 as reconstructed. (38)

" 717 " class 2-4-0 passenger engine No. 717 as rebuilt at Swindon. (39)

Chapter Three

GEORGE ARMSTRONG AND THE WOLVERHAMPTON ENGINES

W HEN Joseph Armstrong moved to Swindon in 1864, it was to an entirely broad-gauge centre. He left his brother, George, in charge of the standard-gauge locomotives and their running and maintenance, with William Dean as his Assistant and Manager of Stafford Road Works. The territory then covered by the standard gauge could be roughly described as a triangle, with London, Pontypool Road and Birkenhead as the corners and Wolverhampton as its " capital."

Although Joseph Armstrong carried full responsibility for the Section as Locomotive, Carriage and Wagon Superintendent of the G.W.R., nevertheless he permitted his brother George to exercise a large measure of independence in the conduct of affairs, so that he was virtually free to create a regime of his own, with the result that Wolverhampton developed its own standards and practices. The situation was not unlike that of Crewe and Wolverton on the L. & N.W.R. vis-a-vis that company's Northern and Southern Divisions, respectively.

The legacy falling to George Armstrong included a miscellaneous collection of older locomotives acquired through absorption of various small railways, and a number recently built for the G.W.R. by private firms and others from Swindon and Wolverhampton workshops. The older locomotives, which dated from 1840 onwards, came from the Shrewsbury & Chester, Shrewsbury & Birmingham, Birkenhead, Shrewsbury & Hereford and West Midland Railways. These locomotives were of various types, few engines were alike and they had been built by several makers; many were unsatisfactory or unsuitable and were scrapped and replaced by new construction in the course of a few years. Of the 210 acquired, some 30 had been withdrawn by 1864, and the 180 remaining constituted the major maintenance problem facing George Armstrong on taking over.

Of the more recently built engines for the G.W.R., 62 came from private firms, 38 of them to Gooch's Swindon design and 24 to Beyers (Manchester) designs, followed by 10 more from Beyers in 1866. Swindon Works had contributed 54, whilst 28 had been built at Wolverhampton to Joseph Armstrong's design before his departure for Swindon. These 154 locomotives being comparatively new, their upkeep was a much easier task.

As regards the older locomotives, the policy here was to rebuild when major repairs became necessary, bringing in standard boilers, cylinders and various details and altering the wheelbase where needed to suit the length of barrel and firebox in the new boilers. In cases where this could not be suitably carried out, the locomotive was scrapped and replaced by new, or almost entirely new, construction; or perhaps by locomotives to a new

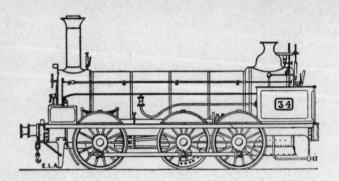

Fig. 29

*Former S. & C.
Crampton 0-6-0
No. 34 as rebuilt*

design of another type altogether. Some had been dealt with in this way prior to 1864.

The first instance after George Armstrong took over was in 1866, when two former S. & C.R. locomotives of Crampton type, Nos. 34 and 35, were reconstructed as 0-6-0 type goods engines of the long boiler type with firebox behind the trailing axle. There followed the reconstruction of two ex-Birkenhead Railway 2-4-0 locomotives, Nos. 108 and 109, with inside bearings, some parts of which were brought in again. Many other such cases were dealt with in the years following.

The first new engines to George Armstrong's design appeared in 1866. They were double-framed 2-4-0-type tender engines with domed, flush top boilers, Nos. 106-11 and 372-7, twelve in all. Except for the boiler, the design was a repetition of his brother's " No. 111 " class of 1863. From 1867 to 1871 he continued with the building of his brother's design of double-framed saddle tanks of " No. 302 " class, but the outside frame was no longer slotted, being cut away between wheels.

Contemporary with these engines were George Armstrong's 0-4-2-type saddle tanks for local passenger train working: they had 15 in. by 24 in. cylinders and 5 ft. driving wheels, and inside bearings throughout. After some 50 had been built, the design was amended in 1870 and those following appeared as side tank engines and with wheelbase increased to 15 ft.; this construction was carried on until 1885. The earlier saddle tanks were

Fig. 30

*George Armstrong's
2-4-0 No. 108*

rebuilt from 1870 as side tanks and their wheelbase increased so as to fall into line with the later engines.   They were renumbered from 517 onwards and so, together with the later construction, constituted the famous " 517 " class of passenger tanks.   This numerous class was in time distributed over' the entire G.W.R. system and operated local and branch services for a great number of years.   Their cylinders were increased to 16 in. by 24 in. and thicker tyres brought the diameter of the driving wheels to 5 ft. 2 in.   From about 1885 onwards most of them were altered to have outside bearings to the trailing wheels, so clearing the footplate of the obstruction caused by the presence of helical or volute spring gear.   A further ten engines of this description completed the series in 1895.

These little engines were most efficient, and their overall coal consumption on local traffic with numerous stops and inclusive of stand-by losses was very low.   In November, 1901, I recorded in my notebook that their consumption in pounds of coal per mile, as published on the coal sheets exhibited at Stafford Road sheds, was no more than 31½ on the average.   The class has been perpetuated in recent times by new construction, as a modernised version on the same lines—a great testimony to their original designer.

Over the period 1872-1875, there was a complete renewal of the Beyer single-wheelers, Nos. 69-76, of Gooch design built in 1855.   They had been used in 1861 to inaugurate the Paddington-Birkenhead services as between London and Wolverhampton, but had been superseded on this run by the more powerful Sharp, Stewart single-wheelers, Nos. 157-166, also of Gooch design, in 1862.   The latter, in turn, had been displaced by the new and larger Swindon-built " Sir Daniel " class of 1866.

The Wolverhampton renewals of the 69 class had new sandwich frames, wheels, and 17 in. by 24 in. cylinders, and a domed flush top boiler of generous heating surface, while Stephenson link motion was adopted in place of the Gooch.

	Beyer as built	Wolverhampton renewal	" Sir Daniel " class
Cylinders, in.	15½×22	17×24	17×24
Wheels, driving, ft./in.	6 6	6 6	7 0
Wheels, leading and trailing, ft./in.	4 0	4 0	4 0
Wheelbase, l. to d., ft./in.	8 0	9 0	7 8
" d. to t., ft./in.	7 6	8 0	8 4
Boiler, h.s., sq. ft.	1112	1304	1203
Valve motion	Gooch	Steph enson	
Adhesive weight, tons/cwt.	11 13	12 13	14 0

These locomotives as renewed were an advance on the " Sir Daniels " by reason of more heating surface and smaller driving wheels, and they proved most successful.   After conversion of the South Wales line from broad to standard. gauge in 1872, they were transferred to Swindon and Neath and used for working South Wales trains via Gloucester, until the opening of the Severn Tunnel diverted the working.   They were subsequently rebuilt at Swindon as 2-4-0 type engines with sandwich frames, and were then stationed at Trowbridge, where they continued to give good service for many years.

At the same time Wolverhampton undertook complete renewal of the Swindon-built goods engines of Gooch's design. Nos. 57 to 68.   They were reconstructed with larger cylinders, Stephenson link motion, new sandwich frames with increased wheelbase and a flush top boiler with dome.   Nos. 60 and 67 were, however, renewed as saddle tanks; they were rebuilt as tender engines some years later.

	Swindon as rebuilt	Wolverhampton as rebuilt
Cylinders, in.	15½ × 22	17 × 24
Wheels, ft./in.	5 0	5 0
Wheelbase, ft./in.	15 6	15 8
Boiler, h.s., sq. ft.	1219	1184
Valve motion	Gooch	Stephenson
Adhesive weight, tons/cwt.	29 12	31 12

The only 0-6-0 type side tanks to be built at Stafford Road Works, Nos. 633-44, appeared in 1871-72. They had inside frames, 16 in. by 24 in. cylinders and 4 ft. 6½ in. wheels, and a tank capacity of 1,000 gallons.   After working in South Wales and at various stations for a period of 30 years, they were fitted with condensing gear at Swindon and sent to work goods trains over the Metropolitan Railway in London.   Commencing with No. 645 in 1872, more engines of the same design followed, but these and all subsequent ones were built with saddle tanks extending over the length of the boiler and having a capacity of 1,000 gal.   Being inside-framed, these engines were 3½ tons lighter than the contemporary Swindon-built double-framed 0-6-0 saddle tanks; the latter's tank capacity was no more than 860 gal., which limited their range of action.

When subsequently rebuilt, the Wolverhampton engines had their cylinders enlarged to 17 in. by 24 in. and the saddle tanks were extended over the smokebox, making them full length and bringing them into line with later construction, the " 1501 " class, built in large numbers for use in the Northern Division on local goods trains.   They even worked passenger trains on branch lines, such as Ruabon to Dolgelley or Festiniog.

The first batch of the Wolverhampton shunting tanks appeared in 1874-76, Nos. 850-73 and 978-98.   They had 4 ft. wheels and, at first, 15 in. by 24 in. cylinders, subsequently enlarged to 16 in.   The 3 ft. 6 in. diameter boiler had a raised firebox casing and carried a flat dome over the firebox on which Adams-type safety valves were mounted.   The full length saddle tank carried 640 gal.   When rebuilt at Swindon from 1889 onwards, the new boiler had the dome in the normal position on the boiler barrel.   The second batch of shunters, which followed in 1876-77, Nos. 1216-27, had 16 in. by 24 in. cylinders, but the wheels were of cast iron with " I " section spokes, as developed by Webb at Crewe.   The boilers had the dome in the normal position on the middle ring of the barrel.   Construction of this type was resumed in 1881 and continued steadily for a period of over 20 years.

After the death of Joseph Armstrong in 1877, William Dean succeeded him as Locomotive, Carriage and Wagon Superintendent in June of that year.   He perpetuated the tacit understanding by which George Armstrong, his former chief, enjoyed a virtual independence in the Northern Division, and this continued for 20 years more.

During 1877-80, the 0-6-0 mineral engines of Gooch's design, Nos. 79-90, were dealt with similarly to previous classes to improve their capacity to run

Pontypool Road-Birkenhead coal trains. They received new sandwich frames with increased wheelbase, larger cylinders, Stephenson link motion and new flush top boilers with domes.

	Swindon as built	Wolverhampton, as rebuilt
Cylinders, in.	16×24	17×24
Wheels, ft./in.	4 6	4 6
Wheelbase, l. to d., ft./in.	8 0	7 4
„ d. to t., ft./in.	7 6	8 4
Boiler, h.s., sq. ft.	1214	1184
Valve motion	Gooch	Stephenson
Adhesive weight, tons/cwt	29 16	34 4

The second batch of 0-6-0 mineral engines, Nos. 119-30, were similarly dealt with, but with the exception of No. 122, which was renewed as a tender engine as above; the other eleven emerged as 0-6-0 saddle tanks.

	Swindon, as built	Wolverhampton as renewed
Cylinders, in.		17×24
Wheels, ft./in.		4 7¼
Wheelbase, l. to d., ft./in.	See	7 4
„ d. to t., ft./in.	Nos.	8 4
Boiler, h.s., sq. ft.	79-90	1154
Valve motion	above	Stephenson
Tank capacity, gal.		1000
Adhesive weight, tons/cwt.		44 13

When renewed, these engines were put to work on coal traffic around Pontypool Road.

About the same time, the two Beyer-built 0-6-0 goods engines, Nos. 77 and 78, and four similar engines by Beyers for the West Midland Railway were rebuilt with new cylinders and boilers and so formed a class of six engines all alike. The eight 2-4-0 type engines of Gooch's design built by George England & Co., Nos. 149-156, were the next to be entirely renewed with new frames, cylinders and boilers.

	G. England, as built	Wolverhampton, as renewed
Cylinders, in.	16×24	17×24
Wheels, coupled, ft./in.	6 6	6 6
Wheels, l. and t., ft./in.	4 0	4 0
Wheelbase, l. to d., ft./in.	8 0	8 0
„ d. to t., ft./in.	8 0	8 0
Boiler, h.s., sq. ft.	1240	1297
Adhesive weight, tons/cwt.	21 12	24 5

These engines worked Wolverhampton-Chester trains up to the opening of the Severn Tunnel, when several were used on Shrewsbury-Bristol trains until the increasing weight of trains necessitated more power. They worked latterly on local trains around Shrewsbury, Chester and Crewe.

Thus all the standard-gauge designs of Gooch had been superseded by new and more powerful equivalents built at Wolverhampton, with the exception of the last batches of 0-6-0 goods engines, Nos. 131 to 148 and 310 to 319, all of which had Stephenson link motion in the first place. Most of these ran to the end in their original form, except that the cylinders were increased to 17 in. diameter; but there were afterwards ten renewals of them altogether, to the same dimensions as the " 57 " class as renewed.

The Beyer goods engines, Nos. 322 to 341 and 350 to 359, were all rebuilt at Wolverhampton from 1878 onwards with flush top boilers and 17½ in. by 24 in. cylinders. Six, however, were rebuilt as saddle tank engines with 5 ft. wheels and 17½ in. by 26 in. cylinders, for service in Wolverhampton and Birmingham areas. Some of the tender engines also had a 26 in. stroke.

The locomotives taken over from the West Midland Railway in 1863 were mostly a miscellaneous lot of numerous classes each containing only a few engines, hence many completed their working lives without being rebuilt. Their largest goods engines, however, were fourteen in number and were very powerful for their time, being of the same design as others supplied by Wm. Fairbairn & Son to the Midland Railway at Derby. These engines, Nos. 280-293, worked salt trains from Droitwich to London and goods trains from Worcester to Wolverhampton or to Newport. None was rebuilt and, like other former W.M.R. engines, they remained at work on the section where they were originally used.

The most interesting and notable rebuilding of W.M.R. engines at Wolverhampton was the case of Nos. 209-214 of the 2-2-2 type and Nos. 196-201 of the 2-4-0 type, both of Beyer design. They were all rebuilt to 2-4-0 type in 1877 to form a single class, but, as an experiment, three were converted into 2-4-0 side tank engines for fast passenger working. This was not successful and the three were altered back to tender engines a few years later. This group of twelve engines formed the mainstay of locomotive power on the passenger services from Worcester to Wolverhampton, Oxford or Hereford. As rebuilt, they had 4 ft. diameter leading wheels with outside bearings and 6 ft. coupled wheels with inside bearings; the cylinders were 17 in. by 24 in. and the dome flush top boiler had 1,247 sq. ft. of heating surface.

In 1885 all six engines of Joseph Armstrong's " No. 439 " class of 2-4-0 type, built at Swindon in 1868, were entirely replaced by new construction at Wolverhampton, outside bearings being provided for the leading wheels.

								Swindon, as built	Wolverhampton as renewed
Cylinders, in.	...	...	...	...	...	...	...	16 24	17 24
Wheels, ft./in.	...	...	...	...	...	...	...	6 1	6 2
Wheelbase, l, to d. ft./in.	...	...	...	...	...	...	...	7 3	8 6
„ d. to t., ft./in.	...	...	...	...	...	...	...	8 0	8 6
Boiler, h.s., sq. ft. ...	...	...	...	...	...	...	...	1085	1287
Adhesive weight, tons/cwt.	...	...	...	...	...	...	...	17 14	23 9*

*Adhesive weight 24 tons 6 cwt. when fitted with " Sir Daniel " boiler having raised round top firebox in 1904

The last passenger tender engines to be built at Stafford Road Works were six of the 2-4-0 double-frame type, which appeared in 1889. As far as the cylinders, frames, wheels and motion were concerned, they were a repetition of Joseph Armstrong's " No. 111 " class of 1863, just as the twelve built under George Armstrong in 1866 had been. The boilers, however, were of up-to-date pattern, while the coupling rods of the 1889 lot were of " I " section. Two odd engines of the same type, Nos. 30 and 110, were built in 1886 and 1887 respectively, so that the total number was 26.

The last goods tender engines were three renewals to the same design as the 57 class, Nos. 316-318, constructed in 1890-1. Thereafter all new engines were tank engines and, with the exception of ten 0-4-2 side tanks, they were 0-6-0 saddle tanks.

When locomotive boiler tubes were of copper or brass, the old tubes removed from boilers could be used up as scrap in the brass foundry. With the change to wrought iron and then to mild steel, the value of old tubes as scrap was small, but economic use for them was found in the manufacture of unclimbable fencing, and at Stafford Road Works an isolated piece of ground beside the Victoria Basin line was provided with buildings and plant for the purpose; it was known as " Spike Island ".

Tubes no longer usable on locomotives were sent there, where they were passed through de-scaling rollers and after being cut to a standard length were placed in a jig and one side of one end was sheared with an oblique cut: then it was turned over and the other half sheared. This had the effect of flattening the end while producing a sharp point. The tube was drilled through near top and bottom in a jig and then dropped in a bath of hot tar which penetrated to the interior as well as coating it outside. Tubes were assembled by stringing them on long rods with screwed ends, short pieces cut from odd lengths of tube being used as distance pieces. These sections of fencing were joined together to form boundaries by connecting together with bolts and distance pieces.

At one time this was a thriving industry at Stafford Road and these formidable black tube formations were a conspicuous feature around the bounds of engine shed yards, goods yards, sorting sidings, round the Works and at other places on the company's system wherever an unclimbable rampart was needed in either direction! The supply of tubes fell off with the introduction of safe-ending of tubes to piece on new ends by electric welding, while modern new forms of fencing have appeared, not requiring periodical tarring.

George Armstrong retired at the end of 1896, after being in charge of the Northern Division for over 30 years.

The wide independence which the Division enjoyed was evidenced by many features. For one thing, the locomotives were painted in quite a different style to the Swindon engines, being distinguished by their dark blue-green shade above the frames, picked out in black lines with fine white edging, as also were the boiler bands. Below the frames the colour was red-brown with black edging picked out in vermilion. The chimneys had rolled copper tops of smaller diameter and of more rounded contour than those of Swindon. Stafford Road Works had its own standard boilers, cylinders and other parts. This was apparent when it happened that a class of engine was rebuilt by the two works. The rebuilds of one works had an entirely different appearance from those dealt with by the other, due to use by each of its own standards, style of smokebox door, cab and treatment of splashers, wheel boxes and side platforms, although fundamentally all the locomotives were alike as regards dimensions. The methods of valve setting were also different.

Boilers for the smaller tank engines made at Wolverhampton all had the raised round top firebox casing and domes were placed on the middle of three rings, which were butt-jointed by straps. In the case of the larger boilers for tender engines, these had firebox casings flush with the barrel until 1893, whereafter they too had raised fireboxes. The two-ring telescopic boiler barrel with lap joints came in about 1892. Boiler pressures were mostly 140 lb. per sq. in. At one period fireboxes had a mid-feather, or a pocket in the roof, but these were difficult to keep free of scale in hard water districts and necessitated much repair work, so their use was abandoned latterly. Only one water gauge was provided; in lieu of a second gauge a pair of try cocks were screwed into the firebox back. The top and bottom cocks of the gauge were coupled together, and a rod extending outside the cab had a handle by which the cocks could be promptly and safely shut off in case of a burst glass.

The Armstrongs provided only the minimum of protection from the weather for enginemen. For a long time it was nothing more than a weather-board with a pair of circular windows in it, but later on, wings were added and then a short top covering. It was not until the early 1880s that cabs were adopted generally, but even so suburban services running into Paddington from some distance were operated until recent times by cabless 2-4-0 side tanks, with footplates open to the sky!

In general, however, the practice was to provide tank engines with short cabs giving protection in the forward direction. In bunker-first running there was no more shelter than that which the bunker itself afforded, though in some cases a weatherboard was fixed to the back of the bunker. Contemporary tank engines on the L. & N.W.R., the Midland and other railways had fully enclosed cabs giving protection in either direction of running, in contrast to the G.W.R. practice of open cabs. I made enquiries into the reason for this and it was explained to me that the Armstrongs had been drivers in their younger days and knew full well the rigours of footplate life with little or nothing in the way of protection, and they were inured to it. In declining to provide some shelter, they were asking no more of enginemen than they themselves were accustomed to. They held that in a confined space the products of combustion which at times found their way into a cab were more injurious to health than any severities of the weather could be. This would no doubt have applied with greater force in the days when coke was used as fuel; the deep bed created gas producer conditions and gave off carbon monoxide and sulphurous fumes when the regulator was closed. With coal as fuel and thinner fires, this condition was reduced, but the opinion persisted nevertheless.

This skimpiness as regards cabs became traditional and the G.W.R. has always lagged behind other railways as regards the amenities of the footplate. Tradition, too, has influenced the enginemen in acceptance of the conditions and the situation of the driver on the right-hand side of the cab, notwithstanding that all other railways have moved him to the left, on which side are the signals and station platforms.

In George Armstrong's day, Wolverhampton was the greatest running centre on the Great Western. Besides the three large turntable sheds, Nos. 1, 2 and 3, there were in addition the straight shed adjacent to Stafford Road Junction, on the old S. & B.R. line, and the original broad-gauge shed relaid to standard gauge.

It was also a training centre for engineers to fill positions falling vacant in either of the Works or in the Running Department and its Divisions. Following on Joseph Armstrong's move to Swindon in 1864, many others were called there in after years and the position of Locomotive Running Superintendent was almost monopolised by a succession of men trained at Wolverhampton. The reason for this outflow of personnel lay in the essentially practical nature of the training, due to the predominance of running activities over those of the Works at Stafford Road; the right perspective from the traffic operating aspect was always in view. The function of the Works was seen to be in providing suitable motive power and to recondition it, as required. At places where an opposite policy prevails and the Works is dominant, there is a tendency to regard the running department as the recipient willy-nilly of any fancy designs produced, complete with gadgets, and as a reservoir to provide a steady stream of locomotives for repair in shops to keep the Works regularly and fully employed, regardless of seasonal changes of traffic demands for power.

As it was situated adjacent to an area in which there were a large number of engineering activities, there were plenty of candidates for admission to the Works. Those not absorbed by the G.W.R. after training found jobs with the smaller British railways or on overseas railways; others found employment with engineering firms or industrial activities in the Midland area. Thus there was a good turn-over of men from which selection could be made.

After George Armstrong's departure, his former Works Manager, W. H. Waister, carried on for a few months until he was called to Swindon to become Locomotive Running Superintendent of the G.W.R. Later, in 1897, J. A. Robinson, elder brother of J. G. Robinson, C.M.E. of the Great Central Railway, was appointed to Wolverhampton, but with this change Stafford Road Works began to lose the independence it had always maintained and it came more and more under the domination of Swindon; as time went on this loss became complete about 1902, when G. J. Churchward succeeded William Dean.

In the reorganisation after 1897, one of the first things to receive attention was the training of young men in the shops. Hitherto, there had been openings for pupils to spend three years in the works, passing through a number of shops, also gaining some experience of firing on the footplate and having a short spell in the drawing office. Apprentices were admitted for a course of five years in the works on the payment of a premium; they were referred to as " twenty-five pounders " by their workmates by reason of the sum paid. These young men had to take " pot luck " as regards which shop they were posted to and how often they could get a move to another to widen their experience.

These two grades were abolished and in their place a system for premium apprentices was established, intermediate between the two grades, with improved status and privileges. A five-year course through the various shops was planned and a programme of courses to be taken at evening classes at the technical college during winter months was laid down, so that the practical and theoretical education kept in step as experience was gained.

I was the first to be taken on under the new conditions and so began my period of service with the G.W.R. Engines coming to shops for general repairs at this time were of great variety and included those built under Gooch, Armstrong and Dean. They were mostly those stationed in the Northern and Worcester Divisions, apart from the few engines dealt with in the old O.W. & W.R. shops at Worcester. The latter were painted there in the Wolverhampton blue-green, but they could be distinguished by their painted dome covers instead of polished brass, an old Worcester tradition which had survived.

About 1900 the later Dean classes began to come in—the " Badmintons," for instance. Apart from this, there were interesting visitors to the running sheds; the latest Swindon practices could be studied during the turn-round of such engines as *Bulldog, Waterford, Earl Cawdor,* the 4-6-0 No. 2601, the " 3601 " class double-ender tanks and many others.

Boilers with Belpaire firebox casings began to arrive from Swindon where re-boilering of engines under repair became necessary. A typical case was that of single-wheeler No. 160, which received a " Duke " class boiler with large dome. The smokebox was built-up and extended and contained an " Atbara " type blast pipe, cast iron chimney bell incorporating annular blower and ejector exhaust and cast iron petticoat pipe. The steel chimney with copper top was, however, retained.

New engine construction continued at Stafford Road in the building of 0-6-0 saddle tanks with 4 ft. 1½ in. diameter wheels. During my brief time in the new engine shop a change occurred in 1902. Commencing with No. 2101, the boilers with raised round top fireboxes and domes on the middle of the barrel gave place to domeless boilers from Swindon with Belpaire fireboxes and the safety valve on the barrel. The making of tanks to fit over the flat top firebox casing was an awkward job and resulted in some loss of capacity and in cramped spaces, as I had reason to find out when wriggling in the interior in order to push bolts through for the attachment of fittings outside. This incompatibility of saddle tanks and Belpaire fireboxes was doubtless the reason for the change over to pannier tanks.

By this time the prototypes of Churchward's standard locomotives were running. One of these was No. 115, a 2-6-2 side tank with outside cylinders, 16½ in. by 24 in. and 4 ft. 1½ in. wheels. A batch of ten engines to this design, Nos. 3101-3110, were allocated to Wolverhampton in 1904, the first order for standard locomotives to be placed, though it was closely followed at Swindon by ten to the design of No. 99, a 2-6-2 side tank with 5 ft. 8 in. wheels; these latter were Nos. 3111-3120.

When this took place I was in the drawing office, and detail drawings of the new locomotives were sent up from Swindon for issue to the shops. They were white prints with dark blue lines, and after they had been mounted on linen, we had to paint the sections in appropriate colours according to the material, and tint the elevations, to facilitate the work in shops by greater clarity. This concentration on one detail after another was an excellent means of becoming thoroughly acquainted with the new designs.

The new engine shop at Stafford Road consisted of two pits, side by side, served by a fixed overhead crane with traversing crab. The procedure was to complete the building of the frames with cylinders, drag box, etc., and then to set the framing on two shop bogies so that it would be pushed out of the way to admit the boiler, which had been brought in by means of the traverser outside the shop. When this was lifted by the crane, the framing was moved back so that the boiler could be lowered into place. Later, the engine, completed so far, had to be moved backwards and forwards during the process of wheeling or where crane work was required.

As the new engines of the 2-6-2 type were longer and heavier than the six-wheeled types constructed hitherto, it strained the resources of the shop, but the delivery of the engines to traffic was even more difficult. They were too long, even with buffers removed, to be conveyed by the traverser to the normal out-going road, because of the distance between walls bounding the traverser pit. The only way out was through the middle of the wheel shop opposite, but as it was not in line with the two erecting shop roads, the traverser could not be used as a bridge. Instead, a temporary track with reverse curvature and widened gauge had to be set up over the traverser pit, but as the curves to be negotiated were too sharp in radius, the pony trucks had to be detached and the engine moved on its coupled wheels only. After the middle road of the wheel shop was cleared of obstructions, a gang of labourers with pinch bars moved the engine at a snail's pace to a point in the yard where the Works shunting engine could give a tow. Once on the straight, the two pony trucks were brought along and the engine jacked up to permit their re-attachment.

About the time of the abolition of the broad gauge, it had been proposed to make Wolverhampton the principal locomotive works, with Swindon for carriage and wagon building and repair and for repair of locomotives working in the southern and western sections of the G.W.R. This fell through because a sufficient area of land adjacent to Stafford Road could not be acquired. In the course of time, with the increasing weight and size of engines being turned out from Swindon in the late 1890s, it became evident that the old Shrewsbury & Birmingham Railway shops at Wolverhampton would have to be replaced by modern buildings, and work began about 1900 to clear a sufficient area of land to the west of the old S. & B.R. line to permit this.

The difficulty with the construction of the " 3101 " class served to accentuate the need and the matter was then treated as urgent. F. W. Snell, Chief Draughtsman at Swindon, under whom the famous " A " shop there had been planned and equipped, was posted to Wolverhampton as Works Manager to expedite new and up-to-date shops of the highest class. After he had surveyed the position and was ready to make a start, he took me over to do the preliminary scheming and later execute the plans under his direction. These and the estimates of cost were in due course approved by Swindon and submitted to the Board, but, owing to circumstances which had arisen since the proposal was first mooted, the directors would not authorise the expenditure and the plan was shelved indefinitely. This committal to continued mediocrity came as a shock to all concerned, but in my case, with this dead end reached, I was offered a position in the locomotive drawing office at Swindon, then at the height of its fame, and so departed from the scene.

An order for 20 more 2-6-2 tanks followed on the first ten, but experience with them in service showed that these small standard locomotives would be more generally useful with a 6 in. larger wheel, so Nos. 2161-2180 had 4 ft. 7½ in. diameter coupled wheels and cylinders increased to 17 in. The last one was turned out in 1908, after which the building of new engines at Wolverhampton was abandoned.

A whole generation passed, during which time the Works only dealt with locomotive repairs within the capacity of the plant. In 1929, a grant was obtained for carrying out a part of the scheme for a new works, by the construction of the principal building therein, which included erecting bays, machine, fitting and wheel shops under one roof; the old erecting shop was converted to a boiler repair shop. This was brought into full use early in 1932, so restoring Wolverhampton to front rank for coping with the heaviest locomotives. It was, however, purely a matter of maintenance; the works was but a northern outpost of Swindon. Its rôle was passive and did nothing towards restoring the spirit of enterprise and initiative which characterised it in the days of George Armstrong, a period which has now passed into history.

Chapter Four

WILLIAM DEAN—THE FIRST PHASE, 1877-1895

AFTER the virtual elimination of the broad gauge east of Exeter there followed a long period of some 20 years' quiescence on the Great Western system until the year 1895. The most notable events in it to affect locomotive policy were the opening of the Severn Tunnel to traffic in 1886 and the abolition of the last remaining portion of the broad gauge in 1892.

The building of broad-gauge engines had ceased in 1866, but, due to the scrapping of the older classes as they wore out, there was a continuing shortage of motive power which Armstrong had made good for the time being by converting 15 of his standard-gauge 0-6-0 saddle tanks, giving them longer axles and fixing the wheels outside the double frames, to suit the 7 ft. gauge. Dean converted 35 more of the class over the period 1884-88, together with 20 of Armstrong's standard goods engines, mainly for use in Devon and Cornwall. Thereafter further requirements for the broad gauge were met from Dean's new designs of standard-gauge engines. The fleet of 27 8-ft. single wheelers of the " Iron Duke " class of Gooch's design, however, were kept in being in more or less their original state by partial or complete reconstruction under Armstrong and Dean.

In the period under review, a total of 727 engines for the standard gauge were constructed at Swindon. Of these, 270—that is, no less than three-eighths of the total—were saddle tanks with double frames of a design originating under Armstrong. Dean also continued with Armstrong's 2-4-0 side tanks used on branch and local services and, when fitted with condensing apparatus, on the Metropolitan lines. The later batches were somewhat increased in size and tank capacity; in all 60 were built. Likewise he carried on Armstrong's 2-4-0 type tender engines with inside bearings for the coupled wheels and outside bearings to the leading wheels, but the diameter of the coupled wheels was increased to 6 ft. 6 in. The " 2201 " class built in 1881 had domeless boilers; the " 3232 " class of 1892 had larger boilers with domes and the cylinder diameter increased to $17\frac{1}{2}$ in. Altogether 40 were built.

The innovations introduced by Dean gave rise to the construction of 357 locomotives, which were of greater interest. Whilst the types based on Armstrong's ideas continued to receive boilers with domes, the new designs of Dean were at first domeless until 1884; thereafter domes were placed on the first ring of the boiler barrel and the smokeboxes were made flush with the boiler clothing until about 1886, when the smokebox was enlarged again. When wider steel boiler plates became available, Dean made use of them to construct his boiler barrels with two rings having a lap joint, and he was the first, or one of the first, to do so. Domes were then increased in size and

45

located on the second ring.   Dean was also one of the first to adopt iron
tubes in place of copper or brass tubes; at one period tubes were given a
slight camber upwards, instead of being straight, to allow the tube plates to
" breathe."   Firebox casings had been flush with the boiler barrel, but in
1891 the raised round top of Gooch's day reappeared on the 7 ft. 8 in. single
wheelers.

The first event of note after Dean's accession was the entire reconstruction
of the ten Sharp, Stewart engines, Nos. 157 to 166, supplied by that firm to
the Northern Division in 1861.   These single wheelers were to Gooch's
design and so had sandwich frames.   In carrying this out, Dean was emulat-
ing George Armstrong's replacement of the Beyer single-wheelers of " No.
69 " class at Wolverhampton by more powerful engines in 1872.

The Swindon replacements, however, were classified as new, and the re-
design brought the engines into line with Joseph Armstrong's " Sir Alexander " class, having 18 in. by 24 in. cylinders, 7 ft. wheels and a domeless
boiler with flush top casing.   The main difference lay in the framing, for
Dean took up again the sandwich frame which his predecessor had discarded.
These ten engines were very successful and they shared the work with the
" Sir Alexander " class on the Paddington-Wolverhampton services for a
great many years.

	Sharp Stewart as built	Swindon, as reconstructed
Cylinders, in.	16 × 24	18 × 24
Wheels, driving, ft./in.	7 0	7 0
Wheels, leading and trailing, ft./in.	4 0	4 0
Wheelbase, l. to d., ft./in.	8 0	8 6
„ d. to t., ft./in.	8 0	9 2
Boiler, h.s., sq. ft.	1240	1214
Adhesive weight, tons/cwt.	12 17	16 10

The reason given for the reversion was that the sandwich frame gave
better running on track laid with heavy longitudinal sleepers carrying the
bridge rail.   This was less yielding than a transverse sleepered track and a
framing with some small degree of flexibility was preferable to the stiffer
single-plate frame.

Conversion of gauge had been carried out by cutting off a piece of each
transom between the longitudinal sleepers, and then bringing the sleepers
nearer together.   Thus, together with the lines of mixed gauge, there were
hundreds of miles of this type of permanent way in serviceable condition
which would continue in use for some time before being replaced by new
permanent way with bullhead rails carried in chairs on transverse sleepers.
The completion of this relaying of the main line did not take place before
1897.

The continuous and unyielding support of the bridge rail called for more
flexible springing and G.W.R. locomotives of the period had laminated
springs of the open type; that is to say, the leaves were separated at the
buckle by short pieces of thin plate so that the leaves only made contact at
their extremities, thus reducing the internal friction of the spring.

The sandwich frame was composed of thick planks of hard wood faced
on each side by thin flitch plates of mild steel, the whole being held together

by a multiplicity of small bolts.   I was fortunate enough to take part in the making of a pair of such frames during my apprenticeship at Stafford Road Works, when about the year 1900 renewal had to be made of the frames of one of the 2-4-0 type engines of the " 149 " class originally built by G. England & Company.   This may have been the last occasion on which such frames were ever made.

The method of construction was as follows.   The four flitch plates were drilled and machined as a batch and brought to the erecting shop.   After being painted, one plate was laid flat on trestles and carefully levelled up. The ironwork, such as horns, spring hanger sockets and the distance pieces at the points where this outer frame was secured to the inner one, were laid in position and the other flitch plate placed on top, and the whole bolted together at the ironwork.   Carpenters then came along and fitted slabs of oak in the intervening spaces, after which they used small auger bits to bore pilot holes for the bolts.   Next, a portable rivet fire was brought up and round iron bars, which were an easy fit in the holes in the plate, were heated to bright redness and pushed through the wood, opening out the holes and charring the wood in the vicinity.   Thus the acid in the oak, which might otherwise attack the bolts, was destroyed.   The bolts were driven in and nuts were screwed on the ends and the whole tightened up.   The second pair of plates were laid to the opposite hand, so that all boltheads were on the outer side of each frame.   The sandwich frame had a good deal of lateral flexibility and I used to watch when the Dean single-wheelers approached a crossover road and witness visible deflection and subsequent damped oscillation of the frame in the region of the driving wheels as the engine passed through the points.   This resiliency reduced the shock on the crank axle arising from flange blows at the rail.

The old baulk road, as it was sometimes called, gave quiet running and this feature was carried over to the transverse sleepered track.   The early chaired road had the wooden keys of the chairs on the inner side of the rails, that is in the " four-foot," and the ballast was topped by a layer of screened ash so that the sleepers were covered and only the rails appeared above ground.   This low height of rail above ground and smooth surface seemed to damp out a lot of the noise caused by the passage of trains.   It was commonly said amongst drivers that they got better adhesion for their single-wheelers on the cross sleepers, owing to the springing of the track.

Dean made extensive use of the 0-6-0 saddle tanks, of which he built a large number, as general purpose engines for branch line passenger and goods work; he even put them on long-distance goods trains where traffic conditions permitted stops to be made to take on water, and as far as their fuel supply would allow.   In this he was reverting to the practice of the former Bristol & Exeter and South Devon Railways.

This partiality towards tank engines was shown about 1879 by the conversion of three of the 2-4-0 tender engines rebuilt at Wolverhampton as side tank engines for passenger work. (Fig. 31).   The axle loadings carried by six wheels proved rather too heavy with the required tank capacity, and these engines were altered back to tender engines in a year or so.

In 1880 Dean therefore designed a 4-4-0 type tank engine, No. 1 (Fig. 32), in which the side tanks were carried forward to the smokebox, in order to

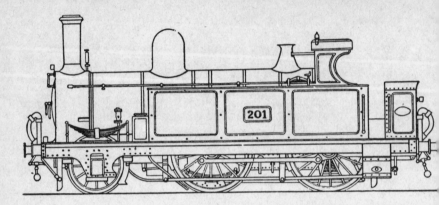

FIG. 31   2-4-0 *tank No.* 201, *converted from* 2-4-0 *tender engine*

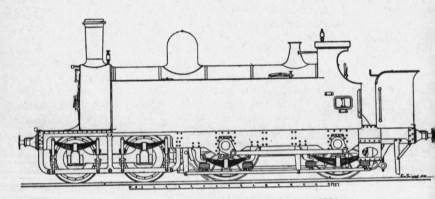

FIG. 32   *Dean* 4-4-0 *tank No.* 1, *built in* 1880

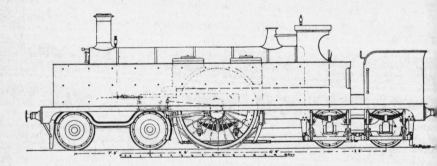

FIG. 33   4-2-4 *tank No.* 9, *with* 7 *ft.* 8 *in. driving wheels*

"717" class 2-4-0 passenger engine No. 726 as rebuilt at Wolverhampton.   It is interesting to compare this with No. 717, the lower illustration on page 32. (39)

"157" class 2-2-2 passenger engine No. 160 as reconstructed at Swindon. (39)

No. 160 as rebuilt at Wolverhampton with Belpaire boiler. (42)

"3501" class engine No. 3510 (originally a 2-4-0T for Severn Tunnel working). (55)

" 3521 " class engine No. 3554. An 0-4-4T rebuilt as a 4-4-0 tender engine. (78)

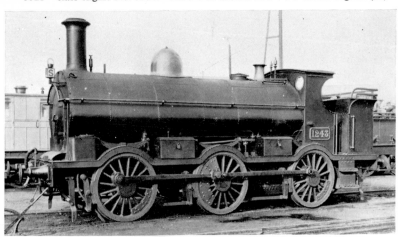

Armstrong Saddle Tank No. 1243 as converted for Broad Gauge. (45)

Armstrong Standard Goods No. 1197 as converted for Broad Gauge. (45)

Dean's " 2301 " class engine No. 2318. (54)

No. 2361. Double-frame series of " 2301 " class. (55)

" 3206 " class engine No. 3213 (as re-boilered and with leading springs above frames). (61)

51

" 3521 " class engine No. 3525 when 0-4-2T type. (60)

" 3521 " class engine No. 3521 as rebuilt to 0-4-4T type. (60)

Deans's single-wheeler No. 10 (62)

increase the tank capacity as much as possible. The leading bogie was centre-less and consisted of a frame outside the wheels carrying the axle-boxes and laminated springs. Attachment to the main frame was through the long spring hangers, which were anchored to a bracket in the form of a large loop bolted to the frame. This arrangement permitted lateral move-ment of the bogie, control being exerted through the inclination of the hangers when displaced from the vertical. Access to the motion for oiling and attention could only be obtained when the engine was over a pit.

The bogie, which had wood centre wheels, was an adaptation of a con-temporary carriage bogie, for I have a note of seeing an eight-wheeled coach built at Swindon in 1880, No. 14974, which had been turned over to the Divisional Engineer's Department at Wolverhampton as a tool van. This had bogies of the same description, with the spring hangers attached to scroll irons fixed to the underframe. Horn plates extending from the under-frame embraced the axleboxes, but left them a large amount of lateral play. This arrangement was evidently the precursor of the famous Dean suspension bogie for carriages. (Fig. 34).

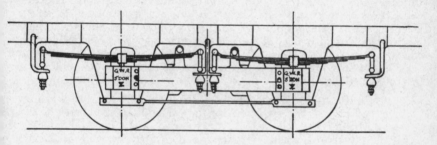

FIG. 34   *The Dean centreless bogie*

Dean's next step was the building of a ten-wheeled locomotive, No. 9 (Fig. 33), to carry full-length side tanks containing no less than 2,500 gal. It was of the 4-2-4 type with 7 ft. 8 in. driving wheels having inside bearings, and was a revival of Pearson's express tank engines of the former Bristol & Exeter Railway. Access to the motion for oiling and inspection was partially improved by locating the Stephenson valve gear outside the driving wheels and using rocking shafts to transmit the motion to slide valves located above the cylinders. The bogie wheels again had wood centres, the leading bogie having inside bearings. The trailing bogie was of the carriage type as fitted to engine No. 1. No. 9 was liable to derailment and never did any useful work, but was set on one side. No. 1 was not satisfactory either and was converted to the 2-4-0 type and the side tanks shortened to normal length. After this essay with tank engines for fast trains, Dean reverted to the tender engine for that purpose.

A chemical laboratory was set up in Swindon Works in 1882. It started in a small way with a qualified analytical chemist and an assistant, but it steadily grew in importance as more chemists were taken on. It was followed by the beginnings of the Testing House for carrying out mechanical strength testing of all kinds. Hitherto simple chemical tests had been carried out by W. H. Stanier, who had followed Dean from Wolverhampton in 1871. At first this work had to be done at his home, until Dean fitted up a small laboratory at the tunnel entrance to the works. With the building of larger schools by the G.W.R. at Sanford Street, the original school building set up by the company in Bristol Street was taken over by Dean as the chemical laboratory.

Crewe Works, at which a Bessemer steel making plant had been set up in 1864, manufactured their own ingots and converted these in their rolling mills into steel rails, tyres, axles, plates, etc. Close chemical and physical tests conducted by a qualified staff were necessary to control the quality of the products. Dean was therefore able to secure the services of a thoroughly experienced man from F. W. Webb, of Crewe, in order to be able to set up the check testing of manufactured products coming into Stores at Swindon.

The initiation of this was supervised by Stanier, nominally Dean's confidential clerk, but actually his right-hand in many ways, being a very versatile man. Stanier inaugurated and conducted the evening classes for apprentices held by the Mechanics' Institute in mathematics, chemistry, mechanics, etc., being a holder of the Board of Education South Kensington Silver Medal, so initiating technical education in Swindon. In 1891 technical education was taken over by the Wilts County Education Committee, and in 1896 the Swindon & North Wilts Technical Institute was founded, later known as " The College."

With the absorption of the Bristol & Exeter and South Devon Railways in 1876, he was largely responsible for the valuation of the plant and stock taken over by the G.W.R.; he reorganised the accounting and office methods as Office Assistant to Dean. Stanier was appointed Stores Superintendent in 1892, and he was Mayor of Swindon in 1908. He was transferred to Paddington in 1915 and finished his career as Assistant to the General Manager.

The next notable event in the early Dean period was the appearance in 1883 of his " 2301 " class standard goods engine, in which a complete change was made, for they had inside frames only. This type was, of course, common on other British railways, but was a new departure on the G.W.R. and by using inside frames and a domeless boiler, Dean was no doubt endeavouring to cheapen the cost of manufacture. The cylinders were 17 in. by 24 in. and the wheels 5 ft. The motion, as originated in Armstrong's *Queen*, had slidebars of the two-bar type but had rectangular guides for the valve gear carried in a box bolted to the motion plate. Batches of the class were turned out at intervals up to 1898.

Construction of this class continued for 14 years, when a total of 280 had been built, but changes in boiler design were made from time to time. The first 20 were domeless, but others following were provided with domes on the first barrel ring and smokeboxes were made flush with the boiler clothing. After that came larger smokeboxes and larger domes set on the second barrel ring. These engines were the first to have modern tenders with the springs immediately over the axleboxes instead of being above the frame. An exception was made in the 20 engines built during 1885-86, for they had double frames, with the laminated springs located below the axle-boxes, and the stroke of the cylinders was increased in this batch only to 26 in. Since these engines cost more to build and were heavier than the inside frame engines, an explanation for this apparent divergence has to be given.

With the continued existence of the broad gauge, standard-gauge engines had to be converted temporarily for use thereon as the old broad-gauge engines were broken up or as the traffic demanded extra power. An inside-framed engine was unsuitable for conversion, hence a potential supply of double-frame engines in case the demands of the broad gauge had to be met. Actually no conversions were carried out on the " 2361 " series of the " 2301 " class.

Contemporary with these tender engines were some saddle tanks with the same dimensions and carrying the same boiler. These 40 engines of the " 1661 " class, with double frames and underhung springs, were also suitable for convertibles, if need be. In addition, there were five 2-4-0 type tender engines, the " 3201 ", or " Stella " class, with the same boiler and dimensions. Just before this, a number of 2-4-0 side tank engines with 5 ft. 1 in. wheels, 17 in. by 26 in. cylinders and having boilers, valve gear and other parts in common with the 0-6-0 tender and saddle tank engines were actually supplied to the broad gauge as convertibles. The coupled wheels were therefore outside the double frames, but the leading wheels had outside bearings carried in additional frame plates.

These engines were intended for mixed traffic duties west of Exeter, but, as the tank capacity was insufficient for non-stop runs between Exeter and Plymouth, some were converted to tender engines. When eventually altered back for standard gauge running, they had all the characteristics of the double-framed engines of the " 2361 " class goods engine except that they were of the 2-4-0 type, as in the case of the " 3201 " class. Thus these and the saddle tanks formed four classes having interchangeable parts. It should be noted that the " 3001 " class single-wheelers of 1891 also had double frames with underhung laminated springs, and of 30 built eight were converted for broad gauge. This form of construction was therefore a feature of all Dean's convertibles.

I always had an affection for the " 2301 " class, as it was on one of these engines that my first experience of driving was gained in my apprenticeship days. The occasion was the running of a special train on a Sunday which included a travelling crane and a crocodile wagon carrying a balloon tank, which was to be set on prepared foundations at Oldbury for use of the branch line engine. The driver invited me to take over on the return trip to Wolver-hampton at night, and while he kept a look-out I endeavoured to spot the signals for myself. In those days the signal arms on the G.W.R. carried only red glasses whether for stop signals or distants, and when they dropped to clear a white light was exhibited. In an industrialised area with much street and other lighting it was difficult to pick out the white light at a dis-tance, especially as approaching passenger trains carried white lights for the headcode. More confusion was to be found where the L. & N.W.R. lines intersected, as their signal lights showed green in the off position where intermediate signalboxes had been cut out on a Sunday, and these could be mistaken for the green or combination of green and white lights in the head codes carried by G.W.R. goods trains.

I mention this matter in passing as showing the aspect from the footplate at night at the turn of the century. In 1903 a standard headcode composed of white lights only was drawn up, which the G.W.R. and most of the other railway companies adopted, and the use of green and purple lights on locomotives was abolished. The G.W.R. then added green glasses to their signal arms. Amber in place of red on distant signals is a comparatively recent change.

In the 1914-18 war a large number of the " 2301 " class were sent overseas for use on the military railways, both on the Continent and in the Middle East. Afterwards, those not destroyed or sold were brought home and put back into service. When the second world war broke out in 1939, the veteran " 2301 " class once more went overseas, no fewer than 109 of them going into action. Other companies' 0-6-0 engines were sent to the Great Western to take their place. It speaks volumes for the soundness and reliability of Dean's design that the choice fell on the " 2301 " class on each occasion. They were veritable " war horses " and their part in the national effort should not go unrecorded.

All G.W.R. engines were fitted with a powerful steam brake. On tender engines the action was simple and direct, as a pair of horizontal cylinders were used, each being fixed behind the trailing footstep on either side and in line with the wheels. Steam was admitted at the front end and pushed out the piston rod, which carried a wide crossbar, at the rear. The brake rods were in pairs and were attached at each end of the cross-bar so that they straddled the cylinder and passed forward on either side of each wheel to connect to the bottom of each brake hanger fixed in front of the wheels; the only connections between the independent sets on each side of the engine were light rods attached to the bottom of the hangers to take up the outward thrust of the blocks due to the coning of the tyre treads.

Where there was a hand brake and brake shaft, as on tank engines and on tenders, a single vertical cylinder carried on trunnions was used. This pulled upwards on application of steam and was consequently fitted with a piston rod packing gland. In the case of tenders, steam was supplied through an armoured rubber hose between engine and tender.

When continuous brakes began to be fitted to trains, the G.W.R. gave trial to the Sanders vacuum brake in 1876, and then made more extensive use of its improved form in the Sanders-Bolitho brake. Whilst approving of the principle on which it worked, Dean thought that it was capable of improvement and in 1880 decided that the G.W.R. should design a brake of their own. The man entrusted with this work was Joseph Armstrong, a son of Dean's former chief, and he combined the steam and vacuum application valves and the ejector in a neat and simple fitting attached to the back of the firebox. The soundness and fitness of this design (Fig. 35) can be judged by its continued use with but minor alterations over some 70 years, and a large number of engines still carry it to-day. In later years Church-

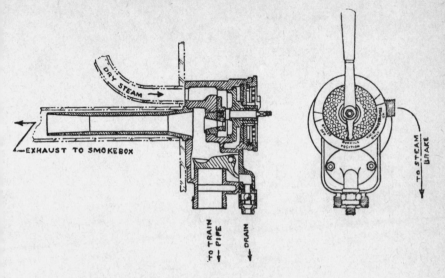

FIG. 35   *Vacuum brake valve*

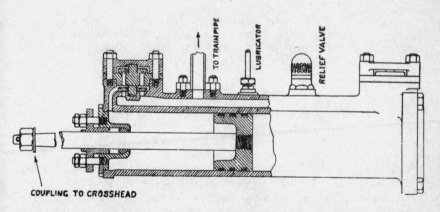

FIG. 36   *Vacuum Pump*

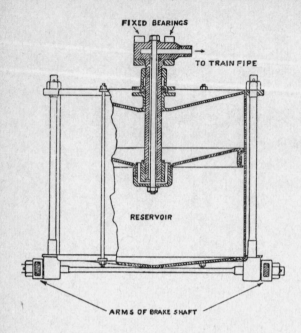

FIXED BEARINGS

TO TRAIN PIPE

RESERVOIR

ARMS OF BRAKE SHAFT

FIG. 37

Vacuum brake cylinder

ward was quoted as saying of Armstrong that " Joe was a careless man and would not be bothered about taking out patents for his designs, with the consequence that others have copied his ideas and he has not received proper credit for them."

The design of the carriage brake cylinder was unusual in that the piston rod was anchored to the underframes by trunnions and the cylinder rode on it, moving upwards to apply the brakes through its direct attachment to the brake shaft. The piston packing was in the form of a rubber band arranged like an hydraulic leather. Air could be drawn past it from the reservoir side of the piston, but the band prevented its return on application of the brake, so that it acted as a non-return valve and made the use of a ball valve for that purpose unnecessary (Fig. 37). G. J. Churchward, then an Assistant to the Carriage Works Manager at Swindon, collaborated with Armstrong in the design, which was perpetuated until 1903 when the more orthodox form of cylinder carried on trunnions took its place, though it still retained the rubber band on the piston. This type of cylinder was also applied to locomotives, commencing with No. 100 in 1902.

As locomotives were equipped with apparatus for operating vacuum brakes on trains they were fitted with a vacuum pump directly driven off one of the main crossheads, to maintain the vacuum while running, a 5 in. diameter pump being used on large wheeled engines and a 4 in. one on small wheeled; even shunting tanks were fitted. By means of this pump a vacuum equivalent to a head of 25 in. of mercury can be maintained, a higher degree than it is economic to attain by use of a small ejector (Fig 36).

In the early 1880s, compounding had been taken up extensively by Webb on the L. & N.W.R. and by Worsdell on the N.E.R. Dean decided to try it and produced two engines of the 2-4-0 type with double frames, Nos. 7 and 8. These were four-cylinder compounds, with the cylinders arranged in tandem inside the frames, so that from the exterior there was little to distinguish them from conventional engines of the type.

No. 8 was built as a convertible for use on the broad gauge, having long axles and coupled wheels outside the double frames. The leading wheels had outside bearings in additional frames, as in the 2-4-0 side tanks. The 22 in. dia. low pressure cylinder was fixed in front of the 14 in. dia. high-pressure cylinder, the l.p. having two piston rods which passed outside the h.p. cylinder casting, so that the crosshead had three piston rods coupled to it. The stroke was 21 in., the coupled wheels 7 ft. in diameter and the boiler pressure was 180 lb. per sq. in. On the other hand, No. 7, which was built for running on the standard gauge, had the l.p. piston rod connected directly to the h.p. piston, passing through an intermediate bush. Whether any benefit was obtained through compounding is not recorded as neither engine was a success from the mechanical aspect. The engines were eventually taken out of traffic and laid aside for future rebuilding.

Important developments occurred on the G.W.R. system from 1887 onwards, and are mentioned because they affected locomotive policy in providing suitable motive power to meet them. The Severn Tunnel had been completed in 1885, but its use was limited at first because additional pumping and ventilating plant had to be installed at Sudbrook. On account of the great length of the tunnel and its approaches in deep cuttings, special safety precautions had to be taken because of the difficulty of reaching trains stranded in the section through any mishap, more especially in the tunnel itself.

Coal trains and ordinary freight were permitted to run provided the wagons contained nothing inflammable or explosive—oil tanks and gun-powder wagons were barred. The approaches and each half of the tunnel were on gradients of 1 in 90 at the northern end and 1 in 100 at the southern, the opposite slopes meeting near the middle of the tunnel, and special instructions had to be given to drivers and guards as to the handling of trains to avoid any snatches that might result in broken couplings as the train passed off and on to the slopes on reaching the short stretch of level separating them. Although the approach roads were laid in new bullhead rail on transverse sleepers, the track through the tunnel itself had 68 lb. bridge rails on longitudinal sleepers. It was known from broad-gauge experience that a derailed wagon in a train might run harmlessly on the longitudinal sleepers while the couplings to wagons fore and aft held it parallel to the rails, whereas on a chaired road much damage would be caused by breaking of chairs and splintering of sleepers, and spreading of the rails in consequence might lead to the rear end of the train being totally derailed and the tunnel blocked.

Local passenger trains which passed through the tunnel were drawn by tank engines fitted with condensing gear, and it was not until 1887, when the Sudbrook plant had been completed and experience gained in working traffic through the tunnel and its approaches, that the first express train service from Paddington to South Wales began, via Bath and Stapleton Road, Bristol. The tunnel, however, was of more value in facilitating communication between South Wales and the West Country, and its full benefit as far as the London end was concerned was not gained until the opening of the line from Wootton Basset to Filton in 1903, which not only gave a short cut, but opened up an alternative route from London to Bristol via Badminton.

One unlooked-for result of the opening of the tunnel was the gradual development of traffic from the North to Bristol. Hitherto, the line from Newport to Shrewsbury and on to Birkenhead had been mainly used for South Wales coal traffic, for which Armstrong's mineral engines had been constructed in 1874. A passenger service began after 1887 in a small way over the Shrewsbury & Hereford Joint Lines and via Abergavenny to join the South Wales line by the Maindee curve, by-passing Newport, thence through the tunnel to Bristol.

The new service then began to build up between Crewe and Bristol; traffic from the North Country, much of which had passed over the Midland Railway to Bristol by way of Derby and Birmingham, was funnelled into Crewe and conveyed by a new artery of communication parallel to the Welsh Border for much of its way, to be dispersed over the West Country from Bristol. The undulating nature of the Shrewsbury & Hereford lines, the mountainous nature of Monmouthshire and the slopes of the Severn Tunnel made it a difficult road to operate. The small 2-4-0 locomotives from Wolverhampton had, in time, to be superseded by more powerful 2-4-0 and 4-4-0 designs from Swindon.

During the 1887-89 period, Dean reverted to the sandwich frame once more. The first to appear were 40 tank engines of the 0-4-2 type, Nos. 3521 to 3560. These had 5 ft. coupled wheels and 17 in. by 24 in. cylinders. Hitherto, Swindon had built only 2-4-0 side tanks and Wolverhampton the 0-4-2 type, but it cannot be said that the result of Dean's departure from custom was a success. The first 20 for use on the standard gauge in the London area had side tanks, but the following batch, built as convertibles for service on the broad gauge in Cornwall, were provided with saddle tanks as customary on that gauge. All these engines had a short coupled wheelbase of 7 ft. and a long distance of 9 ft. 6 in. from driving to trailing wheels, which had a special provision for side play through underhung springs connected to the frame by long shackles. So unsteady was the riding, due to excessive freedom at the trailing end, that the last engine, No. 3560, was provided with a Dean suspension bogie of only 4 ft. 6 in. wheelbase, the 3 ft. 6 in. wheels having wood centres. Short side tanks replaced the saddle and another tank was formed in the coal bunker to compensate. All the other engines were altered to this style, but nevertheless they were liable to derailment at speed or they displaced the track on occasions.

No. 3550 came into the shops at Wolverhampton for repairs during my apprenticeship there. From my notes made then, the altered dimensions to the tanks were as follows—side tanks 8 ft. 6 in. long, 4 ft. deep and 1 ft. 6 in. wide. The coal bunker was 7 ft. 6 in. wide, 4 ft. deep and 4 ft. 6 in. long and contained a tank at the back of the same width, 3 ft. 6 in. deep and 2 ft. 6 in.

long with the front rounded off in the coal space. The connections between tanks were 5 ft. long by 1 ft. 6 in. square.

After general repairs had been carried out, I went on the trial trip; the outward journey was made bunker first and at a moderate speed. My function on such occasions, on reaching the station yard, was to wriggle my way under the engine, and if called upon to tighten up loose bolts or make adjustments under the direction of the chargehand. When all bearings had been found to be running cool, the driver went " hell-for-leather " on the return trip to give the engine a good shake-up—and he succeeded! Although I have travelled extensively since on all kinds of engines and at speeds over 100 m.p.h., there was never a trip like this one. It had to be experienced to be believed, for the lateral oscillation was terrific: the motion imparted to those on the footplate could be likened to that of a terrier shaking a rat! The driver, seeing our anxious faces, gave us a reassuring grin, but he did not attempt to ease up before reaching Oxley Sidings. Before these engines could be trusted to perform any worthwhile duty, they had to be rebuilt as 4-4-0 type tender engines for mixed-traffic working.

The next engines to be built with sandwich frames were two of the 2-4-0 type, Nos. 14 and 16, convertibles for use on the broad gauge, the particular task for which they were designed being the operation of the heaviest and fastest trains between Bristol and Swindon without assistance. These powerful locomotives had 7 ft. wheels outside the sandwich frames, 20 in. by 24 in. cylinders and a boiler pressure of 180 lb. per sq. in.

The last engines with sandwich frames were 20 of the 2-4-0 type, the " 3206 " class, with 6 ft. 1½ in. wheels and 18 in. by 24 in. cylinders. Having underhung springs and double frames, this batch was built with an eye to convertibility for broad gauge, if need be. They were known as the " Barnums " because, having good tractive effort and route availability, they were much used at one period to haul the heavy, specially-constructed American-type rolling stock made for conveying Barnum & Bailey's Great Circus and Menagerie from town to town on their tour of the British Isles and the Continent of Europe.

Dean's 2-4-0 type, the " 3232 " class of 1892, comprising 20 engines' were the ultimate enlargement of the genus of inside-framed designs originating in Armstrong's " 439 " class. These, the last and largest, had 6 ft. 6 in. wheels, cylinders 17½ in. by 24 in. and a boiler of increased dimensions. They were much used on the Shrewsbury-Bristol trains via Severn Tunnel at one period.

The G.W.R. was well provided with single-wheelers for passenger services: there were the 8 ft.-wheeled broad-gauge locomotives and for the standard gauge the " Sir Daniel," " Sir Alexander " and the " 157 " classes, besides the 6 ft. 6 in. wheeled " 69 " class as reconstructed at Wolverhampton. But the time was approaching when more powerful motive power would be needed and alteration would take place in design.

Dean made several trials before settling down to a new design. To begin with, the 4-2-4 side tank, No. 9, which had been laid on one side, was used to construct a tender engine of 2-2-2 type in 1884; the 7 ft. 8 in. drivers, outside valve motion and cylinders with valves on top, operated through a rocking shaft, were worked into this tentative design. One disadvantage of this cylinder arrangement was that the valves did not drop off their faces when steam was shut off, as is the case when valves are at the side or below the cylinders. Although the driving wheels had inside bearings, those of the leading and trailing wheels were outside.

In No. 10, a 2-2-2 type which appeared in 1886, the design was more orthodox as it had double plate frames throughout, 7 ft. 8 in. drivers, 18 in. by 26 in. cylinders and a boiler pressure of 150 lb. per sq. in. The novel feature of this engine was the location below the cylinders of the valves, which were directly driven by the link motion. This could be arranged by inclining the centre line of cylinders downwards to the driving centre and

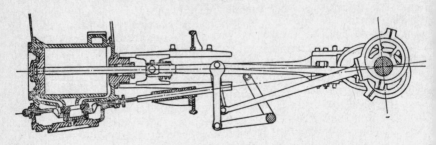

Fig. 38   *Dean's cylinder and valve arrangement*

inclining the centre line of valves and valve motion upwards towards it.* No. 10 was therefore the prototype on which future Dean designs were based—not only single-wheelers, but later on coupled types as well—in the years to follow.

Nos. 9 and 10 were rebuilt at Swindon in 1890 as 7 ft. single-wheelers' but they do not seem to have done anything notable. They came to Wolverhampton for repairs and I remember them mainly for the reversing gear, which was a combination of lever and screw. The reversing gear straddled a barrel-shaped screw having a square thread and this was used in place of the normal sector rack. The lever could be notched up quickly in the usual way and finer adjustment in cut-off effected by use of the handle rotating the screw. From my notes made at the time, the 18 in. by 26 in. cylinders had the valves below, the steam ports being 1¾ in. wide, the exhaust 3¾ in. by 15 in. long. The steam lap was 1⅛ in. No. 9 received a new boiler with Belpaire firebox.

As a result of experience gained, the " 3001 " class of 2-2-2 type were constructed in 1891. They had 7 ft. 8 in. drivers and cylinders 20 in. by 24 in., the largest diameter ever used in a single-wheeler. The boiler had a raised round top firebox casing, a large dome located on the second ring of the barrel, and a pressure of 160 lb. per sq. in. The design was an enlarge-

---

*This arrangement originated with Stroudley on the L.B. S.C.R. It was taken up by James Holden on the G.E.R. soon after he had left Swindon for Stratford. Dean then followed the layout adopted by his former Assistant

ment of No. 10 and had the same arrangement of cylinders and valve gear.
The double frames had underhung springs, as originated in the " 2361 "
series of the standard goods. A total of 30 engines were built, of which
eight were constructed as convertibles for use on the broad gauge, but this
was short-lived for the broad gauge was abolished in the following year and
the convertibles were altered back for standard gauge.

In May, 1892, the broad gauge disappeared. By that time there was
mixed gauge from Paddington to Exeter and from Truro to Penzance, so
that the task presented was to collect on the appointed day all broad-gauge
rolling stock standing between Penzance or St. Ives and Exeter and berth
it in various sidings east of Exeter, to be worked up over the mixed gauge
later, to the reception sidings prepared at Swindon, as circumstances permitted. After collection of the stock, the longitudinal sleepers of the
Exeter-Truro section, the only purely broad gauge stretch left, were brought
in to suit standard gauge by shortening the wooden transoms separating
them. Removal of the broad-gauge rail of mixed gauge everywhere was a
matter for the following months, after which the G.W.R. was left with a
standard-gauge line from Paddington to Penzance almost entirely on
longitudinal sleepers laid with bridge rails. The conversion received a
great deal of publicity in the press and much regret was expressed generally
at the passing of an era, but nowhere was sentiment more keenly roused
than in South Devon and Cornwall. Yet as a feat of engineering it did not
compare with the New Milford-Swindon conversion 20 years earlier, which
had passed almost unnoticed.

With the broad gauge out of the way, a vast long-term programme of
engineering work lay ahead in the doubling of much of the line between
Exeter and Penzance, the replacement of Brunel's numerous wooden viaducts
and strengthening of bridges to carry more powerful locomotives, and
renewal of track throughout with heavy bullhead rails and transverse sleepers.

As a result of the derailment of one of the " 3001 " class single-wheelers
in Box Tunnel due to a broken leading axle, it was thought that too much
weight was being carried on the leading wheels, so it was decided to substitute
a bogie for them. One of conventional type with centre pin carried on a
stretcher between frames would have made it extremely difficult to remove
the steam chest covers and to obtain access to the port faces below the cylinders, but the problem was solved by a modification of the Dean carriage
bogie of the suspension type. For this, four pillars were fixed to the inside
frames, two on each side between the bogie wheels. Two transverse crossbars, carried on the base of pillars on opposite sides, were connected at mid-
length by a box containing the centre block for the bogie pin, which had a
limited amount of side play. The bogie frame had a cross stay on which
an inverted centre pin was fixed. The weight of the engine was transferred
to the bogie by four long suspension bolts anchored at the outer ends of the
two crossbars. By removing the nuts at the bottom of the four pillars, the
entire bogie and its carriers could be run out on lifting the front end of the
engine, leaving the underside of the cylinders clear.

The 30 engines were converted to the 4-2-2 type and at the same time the
20 in. cylinders were reduced to 19 in. Following this, 50 new engines were
built during 1894-99, but here the trailing spring was above the frames and

not underhung. The original 30 were subsequently altered by having their underhung trailing springs brought up above the frames, the cabs being reduced in width to permit this.

Single-wheelers had for long been the principal express passenger engine on English railways with moderately graded roads, but in the early 1880s they declined in favour owing to their limited adhesise weight being insufficient for the growing length and weight of trains, and the coupled engine began to supersede them. A renascence occurred ten years later when six of the English railways resumed building more powerful engines of the 4-2-2 type. Two things permitted this: the heavier rail sections which had been laid in the interim allowed the carriage of greater weight, up to 20 tons, on the driving wheels and the introduction of steam sanding made adhesion more reliable by carrying sand direct to the contact point between wheel and rail, while economy in the use of sand made prolonged periods of sanding possible.

This preference for the single-wheeler was due to its virtues, for it was smoother running, more economical in coal consumption and easier to maintain than the coupled engine. In the Wolverhampton-London link with trains of 7 or 8 bogie coaches of about 200 tons tare, the average for all single-wheelers which I noted from the running shed coal sheets in November, 1901, was about 30 lb. per mile, the lightest, $27\frac{1}{2}$ lb. being recorded for No. 3048 (4-2-2 type); for No. 160 (2-2-2 type), a close second, it was $17\frac{3}{4}$ lb.   The average for 2-4-0 types, 6 ft. and 6 ft. 6 in. wheels, was about $13\frac{1}{2}$ lb. and 4-4-0 types, 5 ft. 8 in. and 6 ft. 8 in., averaged about $35\frac{1}{2}$ lb.

Maintenance was very easy, and I well remember accompanying a fitter into the running shed to deal with a hot box on an engine recently out of shops after general repairs. It was the left-hand outside driving bearing, and after removing the end cover of the box and drawing out the oil tray, all we had to do was to place a jack under the buckle of the laminated spring and raise the axlebox in the horns. The loose slipper which formed the bearing was then lifted over the collar of the journal and taken to the bench, eased by use of a scraper and put back. The whole job did not take more than about half-an-hour. Had this been done to a coupled engine, it would have involved removal of coupling rods, taking down springs and horn ties, eccentric and connecting rods, pipes and brake rods before lifting the engine and running out two pairs of wheels, and then bodily removal of the defective axlebox for attention.

If the inside driving bearing of a single-wheeler ran warm, it could often be attended to by temporarily transferring some weight to the outside bearing by adjustment of the two bearing springs concerned. With the load on the inside box lessened, it was left to the driver to " nurse " it back to normal by using a thicker oil while the engine was put to work on stopping trains. The bearings of the carrying wheels, being outside, could be attended to just as easily as those on the tender.

In starting trains from rest, slipping was quite a normal occurrence with single-wheelers and little notice was taken of the almost noiseless momentary spinning of the one pair of wheels, which the skill acquired by the drivers checked and overcame a few times in getting the train in motion. The slipping of a coupled engine is a noisier affair altogether because a higher steam chest pressure is necessary to overcome the greater adhesion, so that the exhaust pressure is higher, while the whole engine is racked and vibrated by the revolving of the coupled wheels.

The four engines of the 2-4-0 type, Nos. 7, 8, 14 and 16, were entirely reconstructed in 1894 as a 4-4-0 type with 7 ft. 1 in. coupled wheels and 20 in. by 26 in. cylinders. These were the two tandem compounds, which had been laid aside, and the two convertibles with sandwich frames built for Bristol-Swindon service. As reconstructed, they were a coupled version of the " 3001 " class single-wheelers, having the same boiler, bogie and double frames, the curved hump over the driving horns being repeated at the trailing coupled wheels. Known as the " Armstrong " class, these engines were rather over-cylindered and never distinguished themselves as the single-wheelers did, but they were of importance in that they set the pattern for the subsequent 4-4-0 classes over a long period.

With these Dean single-wheelers and their coupled companions, the G.W.R. reached its zenith of graceful and symmetrical locomotive design. Though the later and larger types to come, which were their successors, may have been of more imposing and powerful appearance, nothing has approached the 4-2-2 class of Dean in beauty of line and artistic finish. Gleaming green paintwork on boiler, cab and tender tank, red-brown on wheel boxes, frames and wheels, all lined out in orange-yellow and black, with polished brass dome and safety valve covers, and brass beading on splashers and cab edges, copper-top chimney, and polished ironwork on smokebox door. On the wheel box were the name in brass letters standing out from a black background and a medallion with the company's arms in colour; on the tender side the company's monogram.

The running sheds took a great pride in turning out every engine in a spick-and-span condition: it sustained morale at a high pitch, an asset not measurable in monetary terms and seemingly of no account today.

Chapter Five

THE TRANSITION—DEAN TO CHURCHWARD

THE years 1895 to 1902 are of great interest and importance in witnessing a complete but gradual orientation of traditional G.W.R. design to something entirely different in character. During this period there was much in the way of trial and error in the path of progress. New designs appeared and were further developed; others fell by the wayside after a brief life. In the end the final locomotive design bore no resemblance to anything existing at the commencement of the seven-year period under consideration. At its beginning, Dean's 80 single-wheelers of the " 3001 " class dominated express passenger trains on the easier-graded main lines, while the 280 engines of the " 2301 " class bore the brunt of heavier freight train haulage. Their designer had established his reputation on locomotives such as these, for there were others of his which equally well played their indispensable part in the operation of the system.

Dean had reached the height of his powers, but now change was in the air. From this time onwards the hand of Churchward, Dean's Principal Assistant, begins to show and the influence of his counsel is more and more in evidence as time goes on. With gradually failing health, Dean began to relax his hold of affairs until towards the end Churchward was " the power behind the throne."

One of the greatest obstacles to improvement of train services was removed in 1895 by the abolition of the 10 minutes' stop at Swindon. The terms of the station refreshment room contract, dating from the opening of the line for a period of 100 years, made it compulsory for all trains to stop there to give passengers the opportunity to patronise the refreshment rooms. A large sum by way of compensation had to be paid to the contractors to cancel the agreement. Non-stop running then began with the Paddington-Bristol trains, and this heralded a great awakening which brought about an active, progressive policy for the improvement and acceleration of train services and the opening of new direct lines, for the G.W.R. was once known as the " Great Way Round," owing to its many circuitous routes.

Attention was first given to the line west of Exeter, where track and structures were being strengthened for the running of heavier engines than those used on the broad gauge. While the road beyond Newton Abbot is heavily graded throughout, the portion between that point and Plymouth is the worst section, for the former South Devon Railway was planned by Brunel to work on the atmospheric principle, in which tractive effort was constant and independent of adhesion; thus steeper gradients could be tolerated than is desirable for steam traction, and they were of the order of 1 in 40. This legacy of the past has had its impact on G.W.R. locomotive practice ever since the line was taken over.

During the three years which had elapsed since the broad gauge was abolished, sufficient progress had been made by 1895 for the acceptance of more powerful locomotives from Exeter to Penzance. The first design to appear was the " Duke of Cornwall " class, a 4-4-0 tender engine with 5 ft 7½ in. wheels and 18 in. by 26 in. cylinders. The boiler was based on the " 2301 " class, but had a barrel 9 in. longer and a firebox 6 in. longer. Otherwise the design was characteristic of the " Armstrong " class in having double frames, suspension bogie and cylinders with steam chest below, with valves directly driven by link motion. The bogie and tender wheels, however, had wood centres, as in the case of the " 3521 " class tanks and others. This construction continued until 1897, when 40 engines of the class had been built.

The novel feature of the " Duke " class was the extended smokebox of built-up type, which was fitted inside with a diaphragm plate and netting to arrest sparks, as used in American locomotives of the period. Part of the exhaust steam was conducted back to the tender for feed heating, and feed pumps, driven from the crossheads, delivered hot water to large clack boxes on the sides of the barrel. This system of feed heating, which was also applied to some of the " 3001 " class 4-2-2 engines, had many disadvantages and was soon superseded by the exhaust steam injector, a fitting which has ever since been extensively used on the G.W.R.

By 1897 much of the main line from Paddington to the West had been relaid with transverse sleepers carrying heavy bullhead rails and water troughs had been installed near Goring and at Fox's Wood, near Bristol. By this provision, Dean's single-wheelers were able to operate non-stop trains between Paddington and Exeter via the Bristol relief line and also between Paddington and Newport via the Severn Tunnel. Water softening plant installed for supplying the water troughs greatly reduced the heavy scale formation in boilers of those engines stationed at the Westbourne Park shed which took part of their daily supply of water from the two troughs in question.

The " Duke " class framing, cylinders and motion were the foundation on which a number of developments occurred, mainly in connection with the boilers carried. Building of the first 40 " Dukes " was completed by 1897, and two years later a second batch of 20 was turned out with some minor differences compared to the first 15. The wood centre wheels of bogies and tenders gave place to the ordinary spoked type, and the diameter of the drivers was increased to 5 ft. 8 in. by the use of thicker tyres; the cylinders had longer ports and it was by now possible, due to the easing of weight restriction, to increase the tender capacity from 2,000 to 2,500 gal. The first 15 engines had boilers with flush round top firebox casings, as before, but four others had raised Belpaire fireboxes and carried a pressure of 180 lb. per sq. in. The remaining engine, *Bulldog*, had a larger boiler of the same description, in which the diameter of barrel was increased to obtain more heating surface in the tubes, while the firebox was lengthened from 5 ft. 10 in. to 7 ft. to give more firebox heating surface and increase the grate area from 19 sq. ft. to 23.6 sq. ft. The cab of this engine was extended to the full width and hand rail pillars were carried up to the roof. The left-hand side of the cab had a door in the front so that the enginemen could pass forward. On the opposite side of the cab was a steam reversing gear control, in place of the screw reverser hitherto fitted to the class.

In 1899, one of the 5 ft. 8 in. wheel engines, *Camel*, was provided with a similar but domeless Belpaire boiler, but the new departure here was the cylindrical or " drumhead " type of smokebox carried in a saddle built up from the cylinders. A new form of cast iron chimney took the place of the normal steel chimney with copper top. Frame fractures in the earlier engines led to a strengthening of the frames by giving them straight tops instead of curving them over each axlebox in the form of a hump, so deepening the plate between the coupled wheels, and this applied to new engines from 1900 onwards.

Intermediate in size between the 7 ft. wheeled " Armstrong " and the 5 ft. 8 in. " Duke " classes and contemporary with the second batch of " Dukes " was the " Badminton " class, the first 20 of which appeared in 1897. These had the same characteristics of framing, cylinders and motion as before, but had 6 ft. 8½ in. wheels in conjunction with 18 in. by 26 in. cylinders. They were the first locomotives on the G.W.R. to carry boilers with Belpaire fireboxes.

This type of firebox casing was prevalent on the Continent and it was first adopted in England by the Manchester, Sheffield & Lincolnshire Railway (later the Great Central), whose Gorton Works adjoined Beyer's Gorton Factory in Manchester. Some locomotives with similar fireboxes were on order for the Belgian State Railways at Beyer's, and the M.S. & L.R. designers recognised the good points of Belpaire fireboxes and their direct system of staying, which they saw at their neighbour's works.

The " Badminton " class had a raised firebox and large dome. The heating surface of tubes was 1,175 sq. ft. and that of the firebox 121.6 sq. ft., grate area being 18.3 sq. ft. and pressure 180 lb. per sq. in. Ten of the boilers, however, were fitted with 112 Serve tubes of 2½ in. dia. instead of 244 plain tubes 1⅝ in. dia. The nominal heating surface on the water side was only 830 sq. ft., but the Serve tubes had internal fins to increase heat transmission. In practice these tubes were found to be too rigid and they imposed greater expansion strains on the firebox, and in time were given up

Developments of the 6 ft. 8½ in. wheel engines kept in step with those of the 5 ft. 8 in. and one engine, *Waterford*, was fitted with a boiler of the same dimensions as that supplied for the *Bulldog*. It was, however, domeless and carried a Ramsbottom safety valve on the barrel, while the firebox itself was of steel instead of copper. The cab of this engine was also similar to that of *Bulldog*.

Cast steel wheel centres, which had been provided for the last five engines of the 7 ft. 8 in. single-wheelers, were adopted in the " Badminton " class and their driving wheels had very large crescent-shaped balance weights; this was due to the Stroudley method of counter-balancing. In the normal way the inside and outside cranks are at 180 deg. apart, so that the coupling rod partly balances the connecting rod and the balance weight makes up the difference. In the Stroudley system, the cranks are coincident in angle so that the balance weight has to be large enough to equal the combined weight of the two rods. When standing by themselves with rods removed,

" 3001 " class engine No. 3001 2-2-2 type. (63)

" 3001 " class engine No. 3013 *Great Britain* rebuilt as 4-2-2 type. (63)

" 3031 " class engine No. 3039 *Dreadnought*, 4-2-2 type. (64)

No. 7 *Armstrong*, 4-4-0 type with 7 ft. 1 in. coupled wheels. (65)

" Duke " class engine No. 3281 *Fowey* (the original small tender had wheels with wood centres). (67)

No. 3312 *Bulldog* with larger Belpaire boiler. (67)

No. 3352 *Camel* with drum type smokebox. (68)

"Atbara" class engine No. 3389 *Pretoria*. (73)

"Badminton" class engine No. 3310 *Waterford*. (68)

No. 3292 *Badminton*. (68)

71

No. 36, 4-6-0 freight engine. (73)

No. 2601, 4-6-0 freight engine ("Kruger"). (73)

No. 33, 2-6-0 freight engine.   (Prototype of "Aberdare" class). (74)

this pair of wheels was difficult to handle on the shop floor, and I well remember that it required a gang of men to control the progress of the wheels along the rails.

One locomotive of the " Badminton " class, *Earl Cawdor*, had its tender enlarged at the back to carry a little more water.   This was done to enable the engine to take the Royal Train conveying Queen Victoria from Windsor to Folkestone non-stop, there being no water troughs.   A second engine had the tender capacity similarly enlarged, no doubt to enable it to act as the pilot engine which preceded the Royal Train by ten minutes.

The next developments in the 6 ft. 8½ in. wheel engines were the adoption of straight top frames and a domeless Belpaire boiler carried in a saddle at the smokebox, as on the " Camel."   This, the " Atbara " class, appeared in the year 1900.   Commencing with No. 2571, new engines of the " 2301 " class had extended smokeboxes, and this extension became general when smokeboxes were renewed in 0-6-0, 2-4-0 and other types of existing classes.

As regards freight services, the building of the " 2301 " class, which spanned the years 1883 to 1897, produced a total of 280 engines.   To this was added an equal number of the Armstrong double frame goods, which had been kept up-to-date by re-boilering with improved boilers; and there were also the small-wheeled Armstrong mineral engines of similar design. All these had served their purpose admirably, but with the development that was taking place in passenger services it was felt that more powerful freight engines would become necessary.

The first essay was a 4-6-0 type locomotive, No. 36, which appeared in 1896.   It had 4 ft. 7½ in. coupled wheels, outside frames and a Dean suspension bogie with 2 ft. 8 in. wood centre wheels.   The domed boiler was a large one, having a diameter of 4 ft. 6 in. at the front ring and a barrel 14 ft. long containing 150 Serve tubes of 2½ in. diameter.   The firebox had a raised round top casing which projected from the barrel at the sides, so reverting to broad gauge practice.   In order to accommodate the 5 ft. 10 in. wide firebox, the inside frames were stopped short before the firebox.   This 7 ft. long firebox had a partly inclined grate, with horizontal portions at front and back, giving a grate area of 35.4 sq. ft.; boiler pressure was 165 lb. per sq. in.   The smokebox was of the built-up type and extended, as in the " Duke " class.   Although this pioneer did quite well, the design was not repeated, and, being non-standard, the engine was scrapped within ten years. It was mainly employed between Newport and Swindon via Severn Tunnel, and could haul trains through the tunnel which normally required two locomotives.

Another 4-6-0, No. 2601 (dubbed " Kruger "), appeared in 1899, but it differed widely from No. 36.   It had double frames and 4 ft. 7½ in. coupled wheels, but the Dean bogie had 2 ft. 8 in. spoked wheels and its frames were inside the wheels, so that the suspension links came outside them.   The cylinders were 19 in. in diameter and had the unusually long stroke, for an inside cylinder, of 28 in.   The motion had single slide bars, and piston valves above the cylinders operated by Stephenson link motion through rocking shafts.

More remarkable still was the domeless boiler which, in addition to a raised Belpaire firebox casing, had a combustion chamber 3 ft. 6 in. long between the 10 ft. 6 in. long barrel and the wide firebox first used in No. 36.

The barrel was 4 ft. 8⅞ in. over the front ring and carried 324 tubes 1⅞ in. dia., giving 1,713 sq. ft. of heating surface. To this was added 166.8 sq. ft. of surface in firebox and combustion chamber; the grate area was 32.2 sq. ft. and pressure 190 lb. per sq. in.

The boiler was supported at the front end by a smokebox of built-up type, while it rested at the combustion chamber on a cradle attached to the outside frames. Another unusual feature was the sandbox, which was in the form of a saddle resting on the top of the boiler at the front end. Steps attached to the smokebox were provided to give access for re-filling the box with sand. Instead of laminated springs, nests of helical and volute springs were used in the suspension.

No. 2601 was preceded by a 4-4-0 type tank engine, No. 1490, in the previous year. This had double frames, 4 ft. 7½ in. coupled wheels and a wide firebox with Belpaire top giving a grate area of 20.4 sq. ft., though the cylinders were only 15½ in. by 26 in. The bogie had wood centre wheels and this engine was the first to have pannier tanks. The design was not repeated, and it appears to have been in the nature of a " guinea pig " to try out new departures in design for No. 2601 and others, for the engine was eventually sold. This engine was in service on the Brecon & Merthyr Railway, which sold it to the Cramlington Colliery in 1916; it was scrapped in 1929.

In 1900 appeared No. 33, the prototype of the "Aberdare" goods engine. It was the first of the 2-6-0 type, and having a pony truck at the leading end was more compact and lighter than the two preceding 4-6-0 types. The design was based on the " Atbara " and " Camel " in having double straight top frames and boiler, smokebox, cylinders, motion and axles in common with them. The coupled wheels were 4 ft. 7½ in. dia., and the pony truck with 2 ft. 8 in. wheels had swing links for lateral control. The weight of the pony truck was carried at the centre by a heavy lever pivoted below the cylinders; the opposite end of the lever carried a cross beam connected to the leading spring hangers on each side, and by this means the load was distributed between pony truck and leading coupled wheels.

Another " Kruger," No. 2602, was constructed in the following year, but, instead of being of the 4-6-0 type, it was a 2-6-0, as the result of the satisfactory experience with the pony truck of No. 33. Two years later another eight brought the total to ten, and these clumsy machines were mostly used for heavy coal traffic between South Wales and Swindon via the Severn Tunnel. The boilers gave trouble, the cylinders and motion were unsatisfactory and they were expensive in crank axles. A few of these boilers are still in existence as stationary boilers in Swindon Factory. Most of the engines had a life of three years only and they were replaced by an equal number of the " Aberdare " goods.

No. 33, on the other hand, had proved to be a very sound design, embodying parts well tried out on the 6 ft. 8½ in. and 5 ft. 8 in. 4-4-0 classes, and a batch of 20 of the same design as the prototype made their appearance in 1901.

The smokebox arrangement with the built-up type of box, as in the " Dukes," " Badmintons " and No. 36, etc., in which a steel chimney and bell was used in conjunction with a blast pipe of moderate height and a diaphragm across the smokebox, gave way in the drum type smokebox of the " Camel," " Atbara " and " Aberdare " classes to a cast iron chimney with a cast iron bell, in which an annular blower and ejector exhaust was embodied at the choke. A petticoat pipe was interposed and the blast pipe was shortened; the emission of large sparks was prevented by the presence of a plate bent to a semi-circle behind the blast pipe, which had the effect of tending to equalise the draught over the tube area. This plate was hung from the chimney bell and could be rotated one way or the other when attention to the tubes was necessary. It was later replaced by a plate suspended from a hinged frame so that it could be lifted clear by levers to give access to tubes.

The double-frame construction was continued by the G.W.R. long after it had been given up elsewhere, the main exceptions being the " 2301 " class goods, the 2-4-0 type tender and tank engines built at Swindon and the Wolverhampton tanks, all of which had inside frames. Although the double frame resulted in more weight and higher first cost, it had many advantages. With a 7 in. long bearing inside the driving wheel and an 8 in. outside of it, a total length of bearing of 15 in. resulted on each side of the engine. The short length of inside bearing enabled a 5 in. wide journal to be given to the big end, while permitting crank webs 4½ in. wide. At the same time cylinder centres were wider, so that there was more room available for the steam chest, where it came between cylinders, or alternatively, cylinders up to a diameter of 20 in. could be accommodated when the steam chest was below or above. One disadvantage of the double-framed engine was the greater liability of the crank axle to fracture than in the case of the single framed engine.

For many years I kept records of crank axles either broken or found defective due to the appearance of hair lines indicative of fatigue flaws. I did not compile any statistics, but my general impression was that such defects were about three times more numerous than in the case of axles with inside bearings only, and that the larger the wheel diameter and the longer the stroke, the greater the liability to fracture. The preponderance of weight on the axle was outside the wheels and this would accentuate flange blows at the rail, which were increased by the leverage as wheel diameter increased. This applied to coupled engines, for the single-wheelers were all double framed and there was no basis of comparison; but notwithstanding their larger wheels my impression was that they were not so prone to fractures as the corresponding coupled engines.

The appearance of a hair line indicating an incipient fracture was sufficient to condemn a solid crank axle. With the adoption of built-up crank axles, this expensive renewal was avoided, as a faulty component could be replaced. Bearing areas were increased with this type of axle owing to the absence of radii on journals. But for the advent of the built-up crank axle, the construction of double-framed engines might have been given up earlier than it was.

In 1900 a remarkable departure from established G.W.R. practice occurred with the appearance of No. 11, a 2-4-2 type double-ender side tank engine. This type was much used on the L. & N.W.R. under F. W. Webb for branch and local passenger train working. It was further developed on

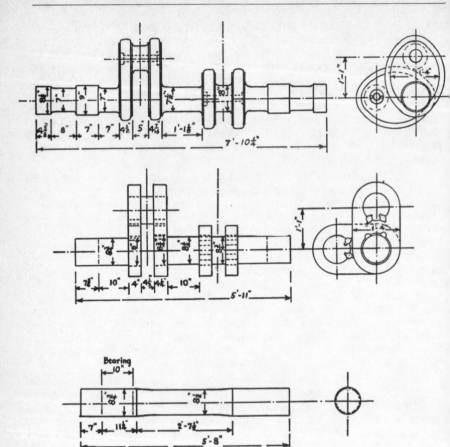

Fig. 39   *Driving axles.   Top: Solid crank axle for double frames.   Centre: Built-up crank axle, 4 Cyl. engine.   Bottom: Driving axle for outside cylinders.*

the Lancashire & Yorkshire Railway by Aspinall and fitted with water pick-up apparatus to extend the use to the working of semi-fast main line trains. No. 11 resembled the latter in having Webb radial axleboxes at the outer ends, steam-operated pick-up in either direction and an enclosed cab, all innovations on the G.W.R.

The boiler was of the domeless Belpaire type, a shortened version of the "Camel" boiler. The chimney and blast-pipe arrangements conformed with that of the "Atbara." The 17 in. by 24 in. cylinders, however, were novel in design in that 8 in. piston valves were located between the cylinder barrels, one above the other, the upper one serving the left hand cylinder and the lower one the right hand. The valves were directly driven by the normal Stephenson gear, the rectangular section guides sliding as usual in the guide box, but the connections to the valve spindles had to be set upwards and downwards respectively and brought over to the centre line of the engine. The piston valve heads had no rings, but were turned with water grooves only and made a close fit in the liners. Theoretically, there was no friction and, therefore, no wear. Large water relief valves were provided on the cylinder covers. Steam reversing gear was fitted inside the right hand frame.

No. 11 was put to work on the local trains between Wolverhampton, Birmingham, Leamington and Stratford-on-Avon. Some time after I saw the engine brought into the shed yard at Stafford Road with both side tanks ripped open from end to end like sardine tins! Apparently the engine had run over the Rowington water troughs near Hatton Junction at a higher speed than usual and the combined air and hydraulic pressure had caused the damage because the vents on top of the tanks were totally inadequate to relieve it. More engines of the class building at Swindon (Nos. 3601-20) had the vents much increased in size in consequence.

The piston valves in this class were not a success, as steam leakage was greater than anticipated. Due to the very slight distortion by heat, the steam chest liners rubbed the heads and more running clearance had to be given. A further batch of engines, Nos. 3621-30, built in 1903, reverted to plain slide valves, and the earlier engines were converted by receiving new cylinders. Some of the " 2721 " class of saddle tanks also had these cylinders, but they were gradually removed although the valves had been changed to " semi-plug " type.

The steaming of the boiler seems to have needed improvement, for No. 3629 had some adjustments made to the height of the petticoat pipe at Wolverhampton in 1904. As this did not produce any improvement, J. A. Robinson, the Divisional Superintendent, obtained a drawing of a Great Central arrangement recommended by his brother, J. G. Robinson, the C.M.E. at Gorton. A chimney, blast-pipe, petticoat and diaphragm were made to this pattern and installed in the engine, but, as nothing further was done in the way of extending the trial to other engines of the class, it can be assumed that it did not have the desired effect.

It was some time in 1901 that single-wheeler No. 3021 *Wigmore Castle* came into the engine shed yard at Stafford Road with wooden templates attached to the frames to represent outside cylinders over the space between the bogie wheels. No. 3021 was used in this way to traverse all the main lines to ensure that the outside profile of the cylinders was everywhere clear of the loading gauge and the edges of station platforms. It was evident to us that something revolutionary was on the drawing boards at Swindon, and speculation inclined to an outsize in single-wheelers having outside cylinders.

A few months later, in 1902, a 4-6-0 type passenger engine which departed from the traditional G.W.R. practice made its appearance. The artistic ornamentation of the graceful Dean designs of the 1890's gave place to stark austerity, and many admirers of the Great Western were even more shocked than they had been by the clumsy lines of the " Kruger." The 4-6-0 had inside plate frames, outside cylinders 18 in. in diameter by the unusually long stroke of 30 in. and high side platforms on the end of which the cab was perched. The Stephenson link motion had rocking shafts to transmit the travel to 6½ in. double-ported piston valves located above the cylinders but inside the frames; reversing was by a long hand lever. The bogie was of the swing link type and the vacuum brake was applied to all wheels, inclusive of the bogie.

The boiler was an enlargement of the " Atbara " design in having a raised Belpaire firebox casing, safety valve on the barrel and a drum form of smokebox carried in a saddle, but the chimney reverted to the steel type with copper top. So much was in line with contemporary American practice that this prototype might be described as an Anglicized version of a typical American 4-6-0.

The decision to substitute the vacuum brake for the steam brake and to apply it to all wheels on this engine and tender arose from the Slough accident of 1900, when an express train from Paddington, drawn by single-wheeler No. 3015, collided with a local train standing at the platform in Slough station. Due to mental aberration, the driver failed to notice the Dolphin and Slough East distant signals at danger, and it was the fireman who looked up after a round of firing and saw through the overbridge the home signal standing against them. He promptly shut the regulator and applied the brakes in full. The driver, then grasping the situation, reversed the engine, re-opened the regulator and applied sand to the rails. The guard reported that his van valve opened fully, and yet with all that done it failed to avoid the violent collision which the provision of quicker acting brakes might have been able to do. The distance from the overbridge to the station was 600 yds. and the brakes were applied in advance of this. A speed of 60 m.p.h. was only reduced to 25 m.p.h. on a level road at the point of collision.

The facts brought out at the enquiry into the accident touched the G.W.R. in a tender spot, as they prided themselves that their version of the vacuum brake was superior to any other in use. As far as the coaching stock was concerned, many experiments were at once made and various proposals examined. Ultimately the sliding brake cylinder gave place in 1903, to one mounted on trunnions and accelerating valves at each cylinder admitted air direct to cylinders in an emergency application. The steam brake on locomotives was very powerful, but a little slow to build up pressure on the initial application when metal surfaces were cold; on a second application it was far more rapid, but this would not occur in an emergency. For these reasons Churchward decreed that in future all large express engines were to be fitted with the vacuum brake to all wheels and a high proportion of weight was to be braked.

During the 1895-1902 period there were three notable cases of rebuilding. The notorious " 3521 " class, the bad riding 0-4-4 side tanks, were converted into useful 4-4-0 tender engines for mixed traffic operation. The cylinders, motion, crank axle, boiler and inside frames were not disturbed, but the trailing end of the frame was shortened and fitted with a drag box; extensions were fixed on the leading end to carry the bogie. The sandwich frames outside were moved back to accommodate driving and trailing axles, instead of leading and driving, shortened at the trailing end, and a new front portion was added. Thus the firebox came between the coupled wheels and the cylinders were over the bogie. The latter was given spoked wheels of smaller diameter.   Of the earlier rebuilds, 14 retained their " 2301 " class boilers, but those later on had new and larger boilers with Belpaire fireboxes, the No. 3 Standard.   These rebuilt engines were very satisfactory and worked various trains, mostly on secondary services in the West of England and the West Midlands.

The much-liked little Wolverhampton 6 ft. 6 in. single-wheelers, the " 69 " class, became too light in adhesive weight for further service, and they were given an extended life by conversion at Swindon into the 2-4-0 type, while retaining their sandwich frames.   They were given names of rivers and became known as the " River " or " Avon " class.   They performed useful work in Somerset and Dorset and in the Oxford area for a further period of years.

Likewise, the adhesive weight of the " Sir Daniel " class, the first Armstrong 7 ft. single-wheelers, was insufficient for the increasing weight of trains.   They were converted into 0-6-0 goods engines with 5 ft. wheels and became equivalent to the Armstrong standard goods, as they had the same boilers, cylinders and motion.   All that was necessary was alteration to the horns of the outside frames to accommodate the changes of wheel diameter and the re-setting of the cylinders and motion to a new inclination.   Those found fit for this extended life gave further useful service over some years; the remainder were scrapped.

In June, 1902, the formal announcement was made of Dean's retirement and the appointment of Churchward to the office of Locomotive, Carriage and Wagon Superintendent.   The development of locomotive design, particularly that of the boilers, had pointed to a new broom at work, and the appearance of many features of American locomotive design were evidences of Churchward's leaning towards it.   This trend, it was said, was influenced by his friendship with A. W. Gibbs of the Pennsylvania Railroad.

Dean's last visit to Wolverhampton was in 1897 to make a presentation on behalf of the staff in the Northern Division to George Armstrong on his retirement as Divisional Superintendent after a period of 33 years.   Although I became one of Dean's premium apprentices in the following year, I never saw him, for all questions that arose were dealt with by Churchward.   From this and other deductions and hearsay, my impression is that Dean's activities declined sharply with the completion of the " Badminton " class in 1899.

The G.W.R. was large enough to find from amongst their own staff all the men necessary to fill the various offices, as they fell vacant by promotions or retirements.   This resulted in a greater length of continuity of policy and tradition than elsewhere, as it was little affected by the grouping of railways in 1923, and continued to the end.   There was no waiting till a vacancy occurred to look round and make selections, but there was a co-ordinated and systematic scheme for promotion of staff from the lowest rungs of the ladder, up to the position of the Chief Officer himself.

Certain qualifications were necessary, for entry into the drawing office, for young men who had served their time in the shops.   Experienced draughtsmen considered suitable for promotion would be drawn upon to fill junior posts in Works or Running as they fell vacant; or men would get sent out as inspectors of material and stationed at such points as South

Wales, Birmingham or Sheffield to inspect steel and other material at makers' works before being accepted for delivery to the Stores Dept.

As there were always more candidates than prospective posts, many would drop off, going to the smaller railways, to those overseas or into other branches of engineering. Of those remaining, men of the right character and temperament would step up from time to time, being given experience, where possible, in two or three departments, such as a changeover from Works to Running, or to Carriage and Wagon, thus broadening their outlook and experience. With the status of Divisional Running Superintendent, Works Manager or Chief Draughtsman attained, the staff position was sufficiently clarified to see who was likely to be considered for final promotion.

In the earlier part of Dean's tenure of office, Joseph Armstrong, a son of the former Locomotive Superintendent, had distinguished himself in connection with the design of the vacuum brake as developed on the G.W.R., in which he was assisted by Churchward. Armstrong was sent to the Running Department at Swindon and afterwards appointed Manager of Stafford Road Works, Wolverhampton. Here, during the next few years, he gave further proofs of his ability and genius and came to be regarded as the likely successor to Dean in due course, but his tragic and untimely death in 1888 ended his career.

Meanwhile, Churchward, who had added to his reputation in the Carriage Works by such matters as developments of axleboxes and axlebox pads, was brought over to the locomotive side, and when he eventually became Works Manager the circumstances pointed to him as the probable successor. On his appointment as Chief Assistant to Dean, his accession to the post of Locomotive, Carriage and Wagon Superintendent was virtually assured.

Chapter Six

THE CHURCHWARD ERA

STANDARDISATION in locomotives had been carried out to some degree by Churchward's predecessors in office, in a general way, by cutting down the number of designs in boilers, cylinders, axles, motion, etc., to the minimum, so that the various locomotive classes had as many as possible of parts in common, and these being interchangeable. Such standardisation, however, had rather waited on events. At times would appear a new design of a certain type which departed in many particulars from what had gone before, and other types which might follow it over a period would as far as possible have as many parts in common with it as their design would allow, and the style of the first would be perpetuated in their characteristics. In five or ten years perhaps, a change of circumstance would call for a fresh design and the process would be repeated.

The advance made in standardisation by Churchward lay in the planning and projection of a limited number of locomotive classes, having outside cylinders and inside frames, and the setting up of a definite scheme of future construction to cover by their use all phases of traffic operation for a long period of years. For these selected types, four standard boilers were needed at the outset to suit the locomotive projected in accordance with overall dimensions, permissible weight and steam generating capacity. There were three driving wheel and two carrying wheel diameters, two cylinder blocks and valve gear, while connecting, coupling and valve rods were alike except as regards length, which was varied to suit each particular type.

Churchward's next step was the building of prototypes of each variety of locomotive to test the design in traffic and so have the opportunity of making final adjustments before proceeding with an order for locomotives in quantity. This ensured that the class, once built, would endure for some length of years without alterations.

While this new development was proceeding, the building of the double-framed types, the " Bulldogs," " Atbaras " and " Aberdares ", continued, as also did the production of further double-ender tanks. The boilers as evolved on all these, however, were superseded by a more advanced design; the cylindrical barrel and straight-sided raised firebox gave place to a barrel having the second of the two barrel rings coned, the bottom of the cone being horizontal and the top sloping upwards from the first barrel ring to the firebox casing. The sides and top of the casing were slightly curved to large radii, while the back plate of the firebox was reduced in width and height so that the sides of the firebox tapered towards the back and there was a small downward inclination of the top. This development gave greater cross section in the region of the firebox tube plate and the first few feet of the tubes where ebullition was greatest; it also increased the steam space.

The reduced back plate was of benefit in the cab and improved the outlook from the cab windows, while saving weight.

Standard boiler No. 1 was derived from that installed in the 4-6-0, No. 100, and was intended for future ten-wheeled locomotives of various types. Standard boiler No. 2 was the developed form of the boiler as used on the *Camel*, " Atbaras " and " Aberdares." Standard boiler No. 2 was a No. 2 boiler with the barrel shortened by 9 in. to suit the double-ender side tanks, and it was used in the later " 3521 " class rebuilds. Standard boiler No. 4 was an enlargement of No. 2 boiler, having the same length of barrel and firebox but the barrel was 6 in. larger in diameter and the firebox top that much wider, due to the adoption of the same throat and back plates for the firebox as for No. 1 boiler. While the grate area was not increased, there was more heating surface and a greater storage of steam and hot water. This boiler was introduced to give more power to certain engines of the " Atbara " and " Aberdare " classes and to increase their adhesive weight on lines where heavier engines could be run.

Ten " Atbara " type built in 1903 carried this boiler, and the engine. were named after cities. This, the " City " class, was an excellent acquisition and took over for a time the operation of the principal trains between London and the West Country. Individual engines of the class created several records in runs with special trains; one, the *City of Truro*, is credited with having attained a maximum speed of 102 m.p.h.* Water troughs laid in at Creech Junction enabled these engines to make non-stop runs between London and Kingswear or Plymouth. Although only ten were built with the No. 4 boiler, their numbers were augmented by re-boilering some of the earlier " Atbaras " with No. 4 boiler in place of the No. 2 originally carried.

In the final form of the standard boilers, Nos. 2, 3 and 4 had the first ring of the barrel shortened so that the coned second ring was lengthened and, consequently, the slope on top was lessened. The No. 1 boiler had both rings coned, there being a continuous slope on top from smokebox tube plate to firebox.

In the standard boilers, the regulators were on the smokebox tube plate and steam was conveyed to it through an internal pipe terminating in two branches which collected steam from the two forward corners of the Belpaire firebox. The success of this firebox, with its direct staying, in reducing boiler maintenance and facilitating removal of scale at wash-outs was such that not only the later Dean designs but also some Armstrong single-wheelers were re-equipped with boilers having Belpaire fireboxes, some domeless, others with domes. In 1903 the movement was intensified by the placing of orders for a large number of domed Belpaire boilers with several locomotive building firms, so that the Armstrong and the Dean goods engines and other classes could be re-boilered with them.

Saddle tanks were unsuitable for use on Belpaire firebox boilers. With the latter's general adoption therefore, the saddle tanks were replaced by a pair of pannier tanks slung from each side of the boiler. These were advantageous in lowering the centre of gravity of the engine somewhat. A much

---

* In 1957 *City of Truro* was brought out of retirement in York Railway Museum where it had been on exhibition since 1931 and restored to service primarily, though not exclusively, for working enthusiasts' specials.

larger balancing pipe was needed between them in order that water might pass quickly from one tank to the other while being filled at a water column, whereas the saddle tank, having one central filling hole, needed only a small pipe to connect the two sides below the boiler.

An event in 1903 which affected locomotive operation was the opening of the Badminton line from Wootton Bassett to Filton. This was 10 miles less and had easier gradients than the route via Bath, so that Paddington-Newport expresses were accelerated by 25 min. and the Newport-London coal trains could be more heavily loaded between Stoke Gifford yard and Swindon.

In 1903, three prototypes were built at Swindon, No. 98, a 4-6-0 passenger engine, a development of No. 100, No. 97, a 2-8-0 heavy freight, and No. 99, a 2-6-2 side tank for mixed traffic operation. In these a further instalment of current American practices was to be observed. Unlike the arrangement in No. 100, the 18 in. by 30 in. cylinders were contained in a pair of iron castings bolted back to back on the centre line of the engine which also included the saddle carrying the smokebox and the steam and exhaust passages. Piston valves of 10 in. dia. with inside admission and long travel were located above the cylinders. These were driven by Stephenson link motion inside the frames through rocking shafts with both arms below the axis, so that the movement was merely transferred from one vertical plane to another without reversal, and not as in the case of No. 100, with arms above and below the axis.

To suit this arrangement of cylinders, American practice had to be drawn upon for the framing at the front end, and each side consisted of a thick rectangular slab attached to the buffer beam at the front end. The back end had to be splayed to a reduced thickness to suit the depth of the main frame plate, a joint between the front and main frames being made immediately

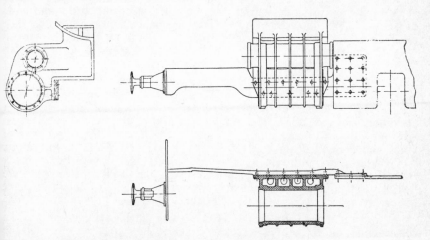

FIG. 40. *The cylinder and frame arrangement of No. 99.*

behind the cylinders. Attachment was by fitted bolts through the over-lapping portions.

No. 97 (now No. 2800 and still in service [1957]) had the standard size of wheels for heavy freight engines, namely 4 ft. 7½ in. dia. With the horizontal centre line of the cylinders intersecting the driving centre, there was insufficient clearance in the load gauge to enable the cylinders to clear it with worn tyres and axlebox crowns. The centre line of cylinders was raised 2½ in. above the driving centre to allow that much clearance in the unworn condition. This was resorted to because Churchward could not tolerate the sight of inclined cylinders on the outside of an engine, which was the alternative. So that the entire motion arrangement could be standardised on all three classes, other than for length of rods, the 2½ in. offset was also applied to the 4-6-0 and the 2-6-2 tank.

The pattern for the cylinders carried alternative saddles for the boilers, one to suit the smokeboxes of Standard boilers Nos. 1 and 4, and the other for Nos. 2 and 3, as these differed in diameter of smokebox and vertical distance between the horizontal centre lines of cylinders and boilers. Engines Nos. 97 and 98 were provided with No. 1 boilers and No. 99 with a No. 2.

The bar frame in the case of No. 98 could pass below the cylinder at buffer beam height owing to the 6 ft. 8½ in. coupled wheels; it was thus straight and therefore subjected to pure compression under buffing shocks. In the case of No. 97, the smaller wheel diameter necessitated a downward set in the frame to pass under the cylinder to join the main frame. This bow shape resulted in bending stress being added to that of compression under buffing shocks, and was thus a source of weakness; but for the 2½ in. offset to the driving centre, it would have been accentuated by that much. To guard against collapse of the front end in serious collisions, the stay plate in line with the slide bar brackets was extended upwards close to, but just clear of, the boiler barrel, so that in the event of the front end being damaged the weight of the forward end of the boiler would be carried on the plate. As the result of experience, stays in the form of round bars were added later at the buffer beams and inclined upwards for attachment to the underside of the smokebox, in order to assist in taking impacts on the buffers. The 2-6-2 tank, having 5 ft. 8 in. coupled wheels, was intermediate between Nos. 97 and 98 as regards cylinder height, the set in the frame being less than for the 2-8-0; nevertheless, the same precautions were taken.

The inability of the bar frame arrangement to stand up as rigidly to heavy shocks as a well-stayed plate frame was recognised and provided for, because of the cheapness and simplicity of the cylinder arrangement it permitted. In manufacture, a pair of identical castings from one pattern were bolted back to back and then dealt with as a unit. The machining of both cylinders and steam chests was done in one setting and the smokebox saddle planed to radius in a subsequent operation. The cylinder block formed a rigid means of taking up the racking due to piston thrusts; there were no joints under steam pressure and the cast iron was highly resistant to corrosion. In the erecting shop the block was set as a unit.

In the case of normal plate construction with outside cylinders, a box-like construction had to be built between frames at the cylinders to take up the racking. A smokebox saddle is set up on this and steam and exhaust pipes with joints under pressure have to be inserted in the box to connect the cylinder passages with the steam pipes and blast pipe in the smokebox; finally, an air-tight smokebox bottom has to be contrived. It is possible to embody all this in a steel casting or a structure built up by welding, but the problems of pipe joints and corrosion remain. In this more expensive construction, the cylinders are machined separately and set individually on the frames. In service, corrosion and leakages of steam joints and air leakages into the smokebox are evils which are liable to occur. By contrast, the drawback of using a bar frame is more than compensated for by the overwhelming advantages gained by the cylinder construction, since the bar frame stands up sufficiently well to normal service conditions, and it is only the occasional heavy impact in an accident which is to be feared. The only classes to suffer habitually from weak front ends were the " 4400 " and " 4500."

Whilst No. 98 took over some of the features of No. 100, Nos. 97 and 99 included the pony truck as fitted to No. 33, and No. 99, the 2-6-2 tank had in addition, at the trailing end, the radial axlebox as used on the double-ender tank, so that these items became standard parts.

By about 1902 there were several stationary locomotive testing plants in use in the U.S.A., and Churchward decided to have a similar plant installed at Swindon. By this means he expected to find out something of the capabilities of his standard types and to make experiments for the purpose of effecting improvements. Since only limited use could be made of this expensive facility for experimental purposes, it was proposed to use it at other times for the purpose of running-in engines coming from the erecting shop after general repairs, instead of taking them out for a run as a trial trip. This would keep the test plant in constant work and save much time and expense spent on taking an engine into traffic; moreover, it would obviate track occupation and so help to justify the capital expenditure. After its installation little use was made of the plant for test purposes once the novelty had worn off; the dynamometer car was found to be indispensable as a means of ascertaining the capabilities of a locomotive in service as a tractor. The proposal for running-in engines after repairs was not pursued after experience had shown that the plant was not a practical substitute for the purpose.

During my years at Swindon I saw very little activity at the plant, and it usually appeared to be dusty and neglected. It was known to the men in the shops as the " hometrainer," by analogy with the device by which keen cyclists of those days could exercise in their own homes on rollers braked to represent the road and air resistances or gradients to be encountered on the road. Occasionally one would see an old goods engine at work on the plant, but its purpose was to revolve the rollers so that air compressors could be driven to supplement the supply, when the shops were short of air. At other times a highly polished express locomotive might be put on for a test, as an object of interest, when engineering societies or important personages were making a tour of the works. In recent times the plant has been resuscitated and modernised after years of desuetude, and new techniques applied, so that with an enlarged scope of test work, greater use is being made of it.

At the period when the prototypes were in the making, the spectacular work of the four-cylinder de Glehn compounds on the French railways was attracting the attention of locomotive engineers everywhere. From 1902 the Great Western had shed former ideas on construction and was starting off with a clean slate. Churchward was determined that it should have the best locomotives which it was practicable to put on rails; that he regarded his initial efforts as tentative proposals to be tried out in service was illustrated by his recommendation to the directors that a French compound should be purchased by the Great Western for an extended trial with engines of his own design. This was agreed to and an order was placed with the constructors at Belfort, France, for a replica of the Atlantic type express passenger engine as running on the Nord Railway, but modified in such minor matters as in bringing the cross-section within the G.W.R. loading gauge, buffing and draw gear, tyre profiles and fitting with the vacuum brake.

Compounding had been under trial on several railways in England since 1880, but without any convincing results. The importation of a highly successful machine from another country was the best means available for determining whether compounding had any real advantages in service as regards express passenger work in particular.

The French locomotive was put into traffic in 1903; it was numbered 102 and given the name *La France*. It had coupled wheels of comparable size to the G.W. 4-6-0 No. 98 and much the same size of boiler as Standard No. 1. The pressure, however, was 227 lb. per sq. in. as against 200 lb. in the No. 1. In anticipation of competitive trials, another 4-6-0 was built, No. 171, and this carried a No. 1 boiler modified for a working pressure of 225 lb. per sq. in., so virtually removing one handicap. The 4-6-0, however, had about 50 per cent more adhesive weight than the 4-4-2, so it was thought desirable to convert No. 171 to the Atlantic type by removal of the trailing coupled wheels and the addition of supplementary frames to carry the outside bearings of a pair of carrying wheels of 4 ft. 1½ in. dia. In this way adhesive weights of the competing engines were brought close together.

While the preliminary trials were taking place, construction in other directions went ahead. Another prototype, No. 115, was built in 1904, a 2-6-2 type side tank; it was a small edition of No. 99, with 16½ in. by 24 in. outside cylinders, 4 ft. 1½ in. coupled wheels and a pony truck at each end, and it had an enclosed cab. The domeless coned boiler with Belpaire firebox was smaller than the previous ones and was known as Standard No. 5, and it had a working pressure of 165 lb. per sq. in. As this engine proved satisfactory, an order for ten was placed on the Stafford Road Works, Wolverhampton, in 1905. These were intended for such jobs as working goods trains on branch lines in Cornwall. Further experience suggested that the engines would be more generally useful if they had larger wheels, so a further twenty were built at Wolverhampton during 1906-08, having 4 ft. 7½ in. coupled wheels and 17 in. dia. cylinders, other dimensions being unaltered.

In 1904 there also appeared No. 3473, the first of ten 4-4-0 type passenger engines with 6 ft. 8½ in. coupled wheels, 18 in. by 30 in. outside cylinders and other parts in common with No. 98, of which it was a shortened version.

carrying a Standard No. 4 boiler in place of the No. 1.   These engines were named after counties in England, Wales and Ireland and were known as the " County " class.

They were followed in 1905 by a tank engine version of the same, a 4-4-2 side tank intended for short-distance passenger trains.   It had a radial axlebox at the trailing end, side tanks and cab much the same as those on No. 99 and a water pick-up for either direction of running.   The boiler carried was, however, Standard No. 2, and not No. 4 as on the tender engines. Although not named, the class was usually referred to as the " County Tank."

In view of the brilliant high speed performances of the " City " class double-framed engines, it is a matter of speculation why the " County " class was built almost concurrently.   Both carried the No. 4 boiler, had 18 in. dia. cylinders and 6 ft. 8½ in. coupled wheels, the main difference being in the stroke of the cylinder, 26 in. in the case of the " City " as against 30 in. in the " County."   The inside cylinders and shorter stroke gave a better and more comfortable riding engine at speed.   In retrospect, the " County " class looks rather a case of synthesis, an assembly of standard parts for the sake of standardisation; it was the least successful of the Churchward designs and the first to disappear in time to come.   Neither did the " County Tank " have a long life, as the 2-6-2 tank was found to be a more generally useful type.

The year 1905 saw the launching of the great programme for re-equipping the G.W.R. with standard types, by the building of the designs embodied in the prototypes Nos. 97 and 99, the 2-8-0 freight engine and the 2-6-2 tank as a beginning.   The standard types were assembled from a selection of standardised component parts.   Thus there was a choice of four boilers and three coupled wheel diameters.   Cylinders were alike and differed only in bore and in radius of saddle and height of saddle above centre line.   The frame arrangements alone differed in determining the type.   On this frame was mounted one of the standard boilers, the cylinders selected having the radius and height of saddle to suit the smokebox diameter of the boiler. Other variations were the lengths of coupling and connecting rods, diameter of pistons and size of vacuum brake cylinder, there being four diameters, 18 in., 22 in., 26 in. and 30 in.

Parts common to all included piston rods, crossheads, 10 in. dia. piston valves, horn blocks, axles, axleboxes, springs, etc.   Valve motion was standard and differed only in length of extension rods, except that the 2-8-0 type had shorter eccentric rods than the others.   Assemblies to complete the design, such as bogie, pony truck or radial axlebox, were standardised.

Distinctive features peculiar to the Great Western in contemporary design, apart from the domeless, coned Belpaire boilers and the cylinder, frame and motion arrangements, were many.   As regards the boiler mount-ings, the regulator fixed on the front side of the smokebox tubeplate, together with its internal collector pipe, was a survival of broad-gauge practice.   It had reappeared in some standard-gauge boilers during the Armstrong and Dean eras, and Churchward once more took it up, but instead of drawing steam through a multiplicity of holes in the collector pipe, he drew it from

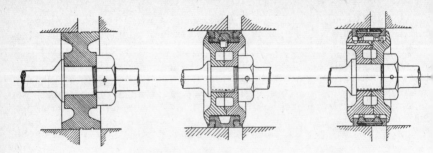

FIG. 41.   *Piston valves—plug, L-ring and semi-plug*

the two front corners of the Belpaire firebox through upward branches from the collector pipe.   He paid great attention to the proportions of the regulator valve and its ports and the jockey valve riding on it, with the consequence that the G.W. engines have been remarkably free from slipping when starting trains, and a high rate of acceleration results, due to the confidence that the drivers have in the control it gives.

It has never been thought necessary to provide more than one water gauge, supplemented by a pair of try cocks.   The top and bottom cocks of the gauge were connected by a rod, and in earlier times had been operated through a handle remote from the gauge by extending a rod to the outside of the cab, so that the cocks could be closed with safety in the event of a broken glass; the try cocks were at one time screwed into the backplate of the firebox, one at working level of the water and the other a few inches above it.   In the modern form of the gauge used on the standard boilers, a vertical column at the back of the shut-off cocks carried the two try cocks, and the handle was brought closer to the gauge on account of greater reliability in the automatic shut-off provided in case of a fractured glass.

The pistons were of box type, with flat sides, being cored out to form internal ribs.   The core holes were screwed and plugged.   The piston rod was screwed into the head with a 1 in 48 taper thread until a given torque was registered.   The projecting end of the rod was then turned flush with the piston and a screw peg inserted half in rod and half in head.

Because of the flat sides of the piston, the cylinder covers were likewise flat internally.   The big end of the connecting rod was solid and provided with a plain gunmetal bush, white metal lined, which was pressed into place with a load of about 12 tons and secured with a ¾ in. set bolt from below. By adopting this type of big end and the flat surfaces of pistons and covers, it was possible to reduce the clearance in the cylinders to ¼ in. each end without risk, so reducing clearance volume.   Two piston rings 1¼ in. wide were originally used, but, due to breakages and short life, ⅝ in. wide rings were tried in pairs in each 1¼ in. groove, with improved results.   It was then found that two ⅝ in. grooves with a single ring in each sufficed.

The Stephenson valve gear had launch-type links, and adjustments were made to the suspension until a very good reading was obtained for both front and back piston strokes.   The unique feature of this gear was the

" 3601 " class engine No. 3611. (75)

[*H. Gordon Tidey*

W. Worcester line train passing Hayes in 1910 behind " 2201 " class 2-4-0 No. 2214. with the
pioneer " 2721 " class 0-6-0 saddle tank shunting in the background. (147)

" City " class engine No. 3433, *City of Bath*. (82)

No. 100 (later named *William Dean*).   The first 4-6-0 passenger engine. (77)

No. 98.   Churchward's prototype 4-6-0 passenger engine. (83)

No. 99, Churchward's prototype 2-6-2T with 5 ft. 8 in. coupled wheels. (83)

[British Railways

No. 115, Churchward's prototype 2-6-2T with 4 ft. 1½ in. coupled wheels. (86)

" 3901 " class engine No. 3908. A " 2301 " class 0-6-0 rebuilt as a 2-6-2T. (103)

Top: "County" class engine No. 3479 *County of Warwick*. (86)

Centre: "County" Tank engine No. 2234, 4-4-2T with 6 ft. 8½ in. coupled wheels. (87)
[*H. Gordon Tidey*

Left: No. 4600 4-4-2T with 5 ft. 8 in. coupled wheels. (137)
[*British Railways*

92

provision of $\frac{1}{8}$ in. negative lead in full gear; i.e., when the piston was at the end of its stroke, the valve had not opened to steam by that amount. As there was no escape for water trapped in the cylinders with the cocks closed, a spring-loaded relief valve was provided in each cylinder cover. The angular advance of the Stephenson motion towards mid-gear resulted in positive lead at shorter cut-offs. This was $\frac{3}{16}$ in. at 25 per cent. on No. 171, but was fixed at $\frac{1}{8}$ in. later.

At first the piston valves had packing rings of American type, the outer spring rings being of L section with a bull ring between them. When the semi-plug valve was brought out in America, it was at once taken up at Swindon, since it had the virtues of the solid plug valves, as used on the 2-4-2 tanks, without their drawbacks. In the semi-plug valve, the rings were pressed outwards to the liners by steam pressure and locked in position there by the wedge rings, so that they automatically adjusted themselves to the bore and floated in it with little friction. This type of valve lent itself to production in the machine shop and required the minimum of work at the fitting bench. The one small disadvantage over other types of piston valve was the rather heavier weight, and larger bush surface was necessary to carry it. (Fig. 41).

In his standard engines, Churchward reverted to the simple hand lever for reversing, though in the " Star " class and the " Saints " from No. 2921, he resumed use of the screw reverser. All these engines had their spring gear compensated throughout, as in American practice. Axles were without collars and with journals 10 in. long for coupled wheels. Axleboxes were of cast steel with pressed-in brasses white metal lined on crown and hub face; horn faces and sides had bronze liners pegged on. Lubrication was from trimmings feed from oil boxes to grooves at 45° either side of centre of crown, and to horn faces. The keeps held an underpad. Churchward's engines were also noteworthy for the brake power, which was 70 per cent. of the weight on coupled wheels.

Building of double-framed engines continued with the 5 ft. 8 in. 4-4-0 type. At the same time the earlier engines of this class began to be re-boilered with the No. 2 long coned standard boiler, and when the *Bulldog* had been so dealt with it gave its name as the class name to all such built or re-boilered with the boiler.

Two years' experience with the running of No. 171 and the French compound No. 102 in the same link had shown that as far as coal consumption went there was little to choose between them. No. 102 was the smoother riding at high speed, but its oil consumption was greater owing to the duplication of cylinders and motion. On the other hand, there remained the question of maintenance, and it was expected that the compound would run a greater mileage between shoppings owing to the division of driving forces over two axles and the greater area of bearing surfaces so obtained. Wider experience was necessary on such outstanding questions and it was decided to extend the trial by the purchase of two more de Glehn compounds. These, however, were replicas of the 4-4-2 type running on the Paris-Orleans Railway and were rather larger in cylinders and boiler than the Nord engine. Delivery from the Belfort Works was made in 1905 and they were given the numbers 103 and 104 and named *President* and *Alliance* respectively.

To compete with them, 19 more of the same construction as No. 171 were turned out from Swindon in that year. All had horn gaps in the main frames for taking trailing coupled wheels if need be, but 13 were put into service as 4-4-2 type, having outside frames added at the trailing end to take carrying wheels; the other six were completed as 4-6-0 type. It is thus clear that, apart from the trials of simple versus compound, there was a parallel trial of types, i.e. the question of 4-4-2 versus 4-6-0 to be settled. To bring about some equality in numbers, ten more 4-6-0 type, Nos. 2901-10 were constructed in 1906.

The situation by 1906 as regards compounding was sufficiently clarified by the experience gained with the three French compounds to determine the next step. The Swindon engines with their high pressure and long valve travel operated by Stephenson motion were just as economical in coal consumption as the de Glehn compounds and therefore there was nothing to be gained by the added complication of compounding. On the other hand, the French engines gave smoother running with their balanced reciprocating masses due to the four cylinders, and there was merit in dividing the driving forces over two axles instead of one.

Another 4-4-2 engine, No. 40, was designed at Swindon to embody these findings. It carried the No. 1 standard boiler and the same wheels as the two-cylinder 4-4-2s, but had plate frames throughout. A pair of $14\frac{1}{4}$ in. by 26 in. outside cylinders was made to overhang the trailing bogie wheels so that it could drive the second pair of coupled wheels without using an undue length of connecting rod, as in the French engines. The $14\frac{1}{4}$ in. by 26 in. inside cylinders driving the first pair of coupled wheels were placed further forward, over the leading bogie wheels, whereas in the French engines they were located between the two pairs of bogie wheels. The reason for the advanced position was to obtain an approximately equal length of connecting rod with that on the outside so that two sets of valve gears could be used to operate four valves with satisfactory results by the mere addition of rocking levers. The outside arms of these levers were slightly longer than the inside arms and were given a backward set through a small angle, instead of being straight. This applied a correction to the valve events and gave closely the same lead, cut-off and release points between inside and outside cylinders.

The valve gear itself presented a problem because the 10 in. long journals of the crank axle necessitated 1 ft. 11 in. centres of inside cylinders and this left insufficient room for the four eccentrics of the normal Stephenson motion in use. It was decided to go ahead on original lines and dispense with eccentrics altogether.

The layout evolved was a modification of the Walschaerts valve gear in which the usual combination lever was driven by a link from the crosshead. The 90° component to rock the quadrant link was, however, derived from the opposite inside crosshead through a reducing linkage, this being possible because the main cranks of the leading coupled axle were at 90° apart in order of rotation, thus taking the place of an eccentric on the axle set at 90° for operating the quadrant link directly through an eccentric rod.

The French engines had their outside Walschaerts gears driven through eccentric rods deriving their movement from return cranks on the crank pins in the second pair of coupled wheels. The gear had only one valve to drive and therefore the scantlings were light and bearing surfaces short, so that the arrangement cleared the loading gauge. Such an arrangement could not be adopted on No. 40 because two valves had to be driven, the inner one through the rocking lever. This would have involved heavier scantlings and wider bearing surfaces for the gear, which to be adequate could not be kept within the loading gauge. Apart from this, there was the objection that, on account of the solid brush type big ends of the connecting rods, the eccentric rod and return crank would have to be dismantled every time a connecting rod or coupling rod had to come off. There was no room between the back of the outside cylinder and the first pair of coupled wheels for a rocking lever to be situated there and it would have had to be in front of the cylinders and driven off the tail end of the valve spindle, in which case lengthening of the spindle by thermal expansion would have affected the setting of the inside valve. In addition, before the outside piston valve could be withdrawn, the rocking lever and its connecting link would have had to be taken down. Finally, it was against G.W.R. tradition to situate valve gear on the outside of an engine. Everything was therefore in favour of the inside valve gear as developed.

In No. 40 a heavy steel casting was inserted in the frames between the outside cylinders, acting as a stay, racking plate and it carried bearings for the various components of the valve gear and reversing gear. The back end of the smokebox was carried in a separate saddle casting which contained steam and exhaust passages linked up to the outside cylinders by short pipe connections. The inside cylinders had a saddle combined in the casting also; this carried the front end of the smokebox. The blast pipe was built up in sections so as to straddle the two saddles and collect the exhaust steam from each.

In service, No. 40, *North Star*, justified the designer's object of amalgamating the best qualities of the Swindon and French designs in a single locomotive. There were, however, some teething troubles, more particularly with the coupling rods. Theoretically, the driving forces in the two pairs of coupled wheels were equal and the sole function of the rods was to maintain the relative main crank positions on each side at 180° to one another, as they carried no load. In practice, unpredictable loading from extraneous sources led to buckling of the rods, and this continued as long as the original I-section rods were put back into use after straightening. Eventually the rods were replaced by others of rectangular cross-section and this cured the trouble, since they could deflect sufficiently without taking up a permanent set.

It was at this period that I was transferred from the drawing office at Stafford Road Works to that at Swindon, and my knowledge of passing events in locomotive development was therefore gained at first hand, as also some information as to what had been going on beforehand.

The Great Western Locomotive Department, which embraced both Works and running sides, was self-contained and self-sufficient. There was no going outside for assistance in any engineering matter, and planning and detail design of running sheds, shops, gas works, water supplies and plant of all kinds was undertaken in the Swindon office. For major building and field works the Civil Engineer's Department usually carried out the construction with their own labour forces, or acted as liaison where contracts for such work were placed on outside firms, in which case they would supervise the job through a resident engineer.

To cover this wide range of activities, the Swindon drawing office was divided into three sections; one for locomotive, carriage and wagon design, the centre section for surveying, levelling, prospecting for water supplies and the making of plans, and the third wing for general engineering. The sections were divided into gangs, usually consisting of a chargeman, two senior draughtsmen, established men on superannuation basis, and one or two juniors whose employment was temporary or conditional; these numbers varied somewhat in different sections. The scheme for training of apprentices in the shops and at the Technical College held out the undertaking that those doing sufficiently well would be taken into the drawing office for a period, and this maintained a flow of juniors. Since vacancies had to be created to maintain the flow, many of these young men were " birds of passage," as they either left of their own accord on finding employment elsewhere, or were given a time limit in which to do so. The select few remained to fill any vacancies and were taken on the permanent staff in course of time.

The office was supervised by a chief draughtsman and two assistants, one for locomotive, carriage and wagon, and the other for the remainder of the activities. The specialised gangs were responsible for various divisions of the work, including one for boilers, tanks, ashpans, etc., another for running gear, i.e. frames, wheels, spring gear, brake gear, etc.; there was one for cylinders and motion, a testing gang and the carriage and wagon gangs.

Elsewhere was the surveying, levelling and plan making, and on the general side the work was divided for cranes, hydraulic plant, works machinery, points and crossings, oil and coal gas works, steelwork construction and building. Ancillary to the drawing office were a materials inspection office and a record office which reviewed and filed all relevant technical publications and books by a very efficient card index system: this office also investigated patents of interest and took out patent specifications when required.

Churchward interested himself in locomotive, carriage and wagon matters, leaving the rest to F. G. Wright, his Chief Assistant, to look after. Besides periodical visits to keep in touch with what was going on in normal drawing office activities, there were occasions when new lines of development or fresh ideas occurred to Churchward or were brought to his notice as suggestions or proposals. In matters of this sort he would have a preliminary discussion in his office with the chief draughtsman to outline the job in view; the latter would then select a suitable draughtsman and get something schemed out on the drawing board. When the job was sufficiently advanced, Churchward would come along, accompanied by the chief draughtsman and his assistant, and settle himself on the draughtsman's stool, with them, the chargeman of the gang and the draughtsman concerned grouped about him. The job as developed would be explained to him point by point, and, when he had thoroughly grasped all the essentials, Churchward would begin to ask questions, make suggestions as to modifications, and listen to what those about him had to say in return. It was the " working committee " in action under a chairman, and the views of all were expressed and listened to. If the piece in question was a casting, Churchward might send for the foreman patternmaker and the foundry foreman to hear their opinions; or in other cases it might be necessary to call in the foreman of the smithy or of the machine shop. Thus any snags in manufacture were avoided at the outset, and constructive criticism by these practical men often led to modifications in the design. If the use of the part in service had to be considered, the running superintendent or one of his assistants would be called in, and he might raise some objections to the matter as it stood and suggest modifications to overcome them. Again, Churchward might enquire what other railways and the French, Germans and Americans did in the matter. The Record Office would then run through their card index and produce volumes of periodicals or books opened at the page, to answer the point in a short time.

Having heard all sides of the matter discussed, Churchward might adjourn the meeting for a day or so for further development or for alterations to be made, or for an alternative scheme to be produced. When satisfied, he would sum up all the pros and cons in an entirely logical way and arrive at a clear-cut decision. One always felt that finality had been reached and the best possible solution had been found. Such was the way in which Swindon design proceeded step by step, and it put the Great Western a decade or more ahead of any other railway in the country as far as locomotives were concerned.

Churchward was a fine figure of a man and his even temperament and dignified bearing suggested the country squire, an impression which his fondness for tweed suitings heightened. He was above all a tactful administrator and a leader of men. He gathered about him by careful selection a technical staff of diversified talents, many of them with academic distinctions. These he inspired with enthusiasm and drew from them their best, and he created the conditions for the growth of good team work and *esprit de corps*.

The eminence attained by Churchward was due to his personality as much as anything. His depth of vision, wonderful grasp of essentials, logical thinking and the intuition by which he seemed to sense what was at the back of the minds of those about him, ensured that the best was always forthcoming. Such items as the taper boiler barrel, Belpaire firebox, longtravel valves, top feed and the firetube superheater had first appeared elsewhere, while the domeless boiler with internal steam collecting pipe and regulator in smokebox was a revival of broad-gauge practice. It was by the recognition of the good points in these details and the careful blending of them into his own designs that success was attained, rather than by the originality of ideas.

As I entered the drawing office in an unconventional manner and was an " unknown quantity " to those already established there, my reception

was a little frigid, and this had to be lived down.   It transpired later that the
course which had been laid down for me was to spend a few months with
each of the locomotive gangs to gain all-round experience.   Eventually I
was established as an independent unit or " one-man gang " to undertake
novel or unusual work outside the routine of the gang system and to explore
the possibilities of various ideas which occurred to Churchward or others.
At the time of my arrival, work was in hand at the drawing office for ten
more of the 4-6-0 type, Nos. 2911-20.   These were to be named after Saints,
but as they differed little from the previous 2901-10 batch, except that the
cylinders were increased to 18⅛ in. dia., there was not much new design
expected.   Also in hand was an order for ten four-cylinder engines, a
development of No. 40, but of the 4-6-0 type.

The trials with the French compounds, the Swindon-built two-cylinder
engines and No. 40 had been carried far enough to enable some conclusions
to be reached.   These were that compounding *per se* was of no advantage
under the running conditions prevailing on the G.W.R., but that there were
a number of constructional features in French design which could be adopted
with advantage, as had been proved with No. 40.   As regards type, the
comparison in service had shown that, while the 4-4-2 was rather the freer
running and more comfortable riding, the consensus of opinion amongst
those operating the locomotives was that the 4-6-0 was to be preferred
because of its greater adhesive weight, which was invaluable on the more
heavily graded sections and made the engine more reliable elsewhere under
adverse weather conditions.

The decision arrived at was that the two-cylinder 4-6-0 should be regarded
as the normal express passenger engine and the 4-4-2 type converted to it,
but that there was an opening for a limited number of the more expensive
four-cylinder engines on heavy, non-stop trains running at high speed.
These would give smoother running, and it was anticipated that they would
compensate for the higher first cost by running a greater mileage between
general repairs than the equivalent two-cylinder design.   Therefore a batch
of ten four-cylinder 4-6-0 engines was put in hand, Nos. 4001-10.   These
had names formerly borne by broad-gauge single-wheelers, and were known
as the " Star " class.

Apart from having a pair of trailing coupled wheels, the " Star " class
differed from No. 40 in another important particular, the arrangement of
valve gear, for the " scissors " gear was dropped in favour of a normal
Walschaerts gear located inside the frames.   The reason for this change
was said to be due to a protest received from Derby about its use.   It was
common talk in the drawing office at the time that a letter on the subject
had been received, but beyond that the exact terms were unknown, and so
the assumption was that the G.W.R. had been accused of making use of
the Deeley valve gear without acknowledgment!

Many years later on I mentioned this matter to my Derby friends, and
they told me that R. M. Deeley had produced many years earlier an arrangement of valve gear similar to that evolved for No. 40.   He brought it to the
notice of his chief, S. W. Johnson, the Locomotive Superintendent, in the
hope that he would give it a trial, but Johnson would have nothing to do

with it, so the scheme was filed away in the drawing office. When in the course of years Deeley became Chief Mechanical Engineer of the Midland Railway, one of his first moves was to design and build a 4-4-0 engine, No. 990, fitted with this gear, but the attention and interest which this novelty might have aroused were damped by the greater furore created by the appearance of No. 40 having a similar gear. A patent was applied for by Deeley in 1905 and this was completed in June, 1906. (Patent No. 16372 of 1905); this period just happened to coincide with the design and construction of the G.W. engine.

The principle of the valve gear was not novel, for those originated earlier by Stevart in Belgium and Lewis and Young in the U.S.A. were examples of cross-connected gears with their movement derived from main cranks at 90° to one another. It was, in fact, a very obvious thing to do, but the only question was whether special circumstances justified its use in place of the simple eccentric or return crank and eccentric rod. As regards subsequent patent claims, in the absence of novelty only particular ways of carrying the principle into effect could be recognised. It was customary at Swindon when producing any new device to take the precaution of instructing the Record Office to investigate whether any patents were in force which might apply to the case in point, in order to avoid infringement. On the assumption that this was done in 1905, Deeley's application would not have come to light as it had not been made public then, so the Swindon design proceeded in an apparently clear field. It so happened that the particular solution reached was so near to that of Deeley that he could claim an infringement.

Whilst no action might be taken as regards No. 40, any further reproduction of the valve gear would be permitted only subject to a royalty being paid if any claim could be established. Faced with this dilemma, Churchward decided to amend the gear as used in No. 40 by converting it to a Walschaerts gear. The general layout together with rocking and reversing levers remained, but the cross-connections to rock the two quadrants were discarded and eccentrics on the crank axle and eccentric rods substituted. To keep down the diameter of the eccentrics as much as possible, the rods were pinned to the side of the quadrants instead of to the foot as normally done when return cranks take the place of eccentrics.

It was a peculiarity of the " scissors " gear that forward running was obtained from the die block in the upper part of the quadrant on one side of the engine and from the lower part of the other quadrant. To actuate this, auxiliary reversing shafts in line with one another had to be used, so that the arm of one shaft lifted as the other lowered, and vice versa. This was brought about by arms moving in opposite directions on the main reversing shaft. In the Walschaerts gear, the two existing reversing shafts moved together, but advantage was taken of the division between the shafts to supply an emergency link, so that in the event of breakdown one reverser could be pinned in mid-gear to keep the piston valves in mid-position by the use of this link.

A drawback to the " scissors " gear was that any breakdown to the motion would totally incapacitate the engine so that it was incapable of moving under its own steam, causing heavy delays to traffic on a main line.

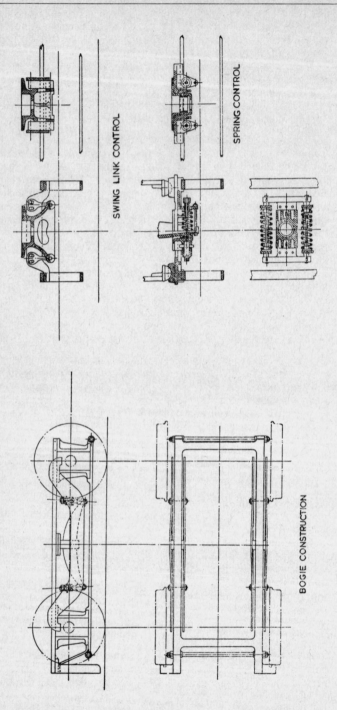

SWING LINK CONTROL

SPRING CONTROL

BOGIE CONSTRUCTION

Fig. 42.   *The Swindon bar frame bogie*

With the provision made in the Walschaerts layout, a breakdown on one side of the engine would put only one half out of action, so that after emergency measures had been taken the engine could be worked away under its own power to the nearest siding or running shed, thus reducing the disorganisation of services caused by delay. Nevertheless, the original gear on No. 40 ran for a number of years with perfectly satisfactory results.

The vogue for things American, which had begun in a small way in 1895, lasted for ten years, but through intimate contact with the de Glehn compounds this was succeeded by an appreciation of some French practices. Apart from the four-cylinder arrangement with its divided drive, the French forked type of big end was adopted for the inside connecting rods. It was, however, the bogie which became general on all 4-6-0, 4-4-0 and other standard locomotives with a leading bogie. (Fig. 42).

The Swindon bogie, which followed the Dean suspension type, was of American origin; it had a rectangular frame of flat bar to which four pairs of pedestals were attached at their upper end and which were braced below by diagonal and horizontal ties. The pairs of pedestals served for horn blocks to carry the axle boxes. The frame carried no weight but merely held the bogie axles in position, as this was done by equalisers spanning the axleboxes on each side. The equalisers were in pairs with a laminated spring between them and the buckle of this butted under the frame. Above the frame at this point a pair of transverse beams on the top of the frame and midway between the wheels carried between them the upper ends of swing links which allowed lateral movement of the bogie. The bogie centre pin was embraced by a centre bearing in the form of a casting provided with legs to carry the lower ends of the links. In the French bogie, weight was transferred to it through ball brackets bolted to the main frames. These hemispheres rested in cups which could slide on flat surfaces provided on the bogie. The centre pin of the engine engaged a centre block on the bogie controlled by a pair of helical springs arranged to act as a compound spring.

The standard G.W.R. bogie was altered to this principle by removing the transverse beams with their swing links and the centre bearing with its bogie centre pin. In place of this, a steel casting was placed on top of the bogie frame and carried the two tables for the sliding cups, the centre block and controlling springs. A new cast-steel bogie centre with bronze bush and ball brackets on the main frames completed the arrangement. Later, this French type of bogie became firmly established in British practice, when it was taken up first by the Southern and then by the London, Midland & Scottish Railways.

Critics of Churchward had for long railed against the angular lines of his standard engines, while his friends tried to persuade him to pay some attention to aesthetics, but he had held out against them and seemed to take a pride in a functional outlook while the liking for American practices lasted. With the turnover to French design, it would appear that he relented somewhat, for I had not been in the drawing office very long before this matter was explained to me and I was instructed to get out sketches to show how a more pleasing appearance could be given to the standard locomotives. Having preconceived notions about what G.W.R. locomotives should look like, I at once put them on paper, taking the 4-6-0 as an instance. In this

I connected the higher and lower levels of the side platforms immediately in front of the cylinders by a single 1 ft. 2 in. radius through 90° and repeated the curve in reverse from the front edge of the cab down to the level of the top of the tender frames, bringing down the cab sides and making the engine foot step match that on the tender. Small cast-iron steps were placed on the curves midway between the levels to give safe footing for the enginemen.

This treatment was much liked, but before making any decision I had to get out alternative schemes with curves of different radii and some with reverse curvatures. It gave me much pleasure when the original scheme was selected, since I had the satisfaction of having supplied the hand and eye which " shaped the ends " of G.W.R. standard locomotives for as long as their construction lasted. This scheme was applied to the " Saints " under construction and also to the " Stars." In the " Saints ", the curved plates and angles in front of the cylinders had to be made detachable by bolts to enable the piston valves to be taken out, but this was unnecessary in the " Stars."

Some of the earlier 4-6-0 engines were eventually brought into line and the 4-4-2s as they were converted. Further batches of the " County " class had curved ends, but the tank engines at the front end only. The name " Saint " class was extended to all 4-6-0s and not confined to the " 2911 " batch. In 1906 a change occurred in painting locomotives, beginning with the " County " tanks. The red-brown, picked out with black and orange-yellow lining, applied to the framing and wheels, gave place to black with orange-yellow lining.

The year 1906 was one of great expansion for the G.W.R. and it had a large influence on the acceleration of the locomotive building programme and increased activities on the running side. The opening of the direct route to the West through Castle Cary and Langport shortened the distance between Reading and Taunton and brought relief to the old main line via Bristol. The completion of Fishguard Harbour works and the connecting branch from the New Milford line, as well as a service of steamships from Fishguard to Rosslare, opened a new route to Southern Ireland, and connecting trains on the other side gave services to Dublin, Waterford, Cork and other places. Boat trains to and from Paddington commenced with this innovation. Ocean liners began to make Fishguard a port of call for passengers from South America, Australia and South Africa in 1908, and in 1909 the Cunard Atlantic liners from New York also called. In connection with them, special mail and boat trains were run from Fishguard to Paddington, stopping at Cardiff for change of engines, and some fine performances were set up, but all this ended with the War in 1914.

A new North to South and West route was opened in 1906 after some improvements had been made to the Banbury-Cheltenham line. Through trains began to operate between Cardiff and Newcastle-on-Tyne via the Great Central branch from Banbury to Woodford which had opened in 1899. In South Wales, the working of the Rhondda & Swansea Bay Railway was taken over. These expansions gave rise to the need for widening the line between Old Oak Common and Paddington. At Old Oak Common, Acton, a large and modern engine shed on the north side of the line was brought into use to replace the Westbourne Park shed swept away by the improvements. This new shed had extensive and complete repair shops and so relieved Swindon Works of some intermediate repairs to locomotives. A large carriage shed and berthing sidings were set up alongside to supplement the West London depôt on the south side of the line. To enable empty trains to cross over from one side to another on the way to and from Paddington, a flyover was constructed over the main line. I well remember the consternation created when a copy of the Civil Engineer's long plan of the permanent way work was unrolled at Swindon and it was realised that for practical reasons the gradients and curves of the flyover would preclude the use of train engines for the movement of empty trains to and from Paddington. I believe a strong protest was lodged, but, if so, it does not seem to have been effective, for these trains have been worked by a shuttle service of tank engines with 100 per cent. of their weight adhesive.

In 1907 another of the re-buildings for which Swindon was noted took place. Suburban tank engines were required and because numbers of the " 2301 " goods class were becoming redundant, twenty of them, Nos. 2491-2510, built in 1896, were converted into 2-6-2 side tanks by frame alteration and the addition of a standard pony truck at each end. A No. 5 standard boiler, side tanks and an enclosed cab completed the job, and they were renumbered 3901-20. These conversions were drafted to the Birmingham area to displace the 2-4-2 double-ender tanks by others with more adhesive weight.

Superheating began in 1906 with the application of the Schmidt fire-tube superheater of the four-fold return bend type to engine No. 2901, *Lady Superior*. This had 24 flue tubes of $4\frac{3}{4}$ in. dia. containing a total of 96 pipes of $1\frac{1}{4}$ in. dia., giving a heating surface of 307 sq. ft. Lubrication was direct to pistons and valves from a force feed mechanical lubricator. It was the first fire-tube pattern of superheater to be used in this country, and so led the way. In the following year, No. 4010, *Western Star*, was fitted with a Cole superheater as used in the U.S.A. This was of the field tube type, with 18 flue tubes of $4\frac{3}{4}$ in. dia. and a total of 72 pipes of $1\frac{1}{4}$ in. dia., giving a heating surface of 269 sq. ft. Based on this, came the first Swindon design of superheater, but the diameter of the pipes was increased to $1\frac{3}{8}$ in. to bring the surface up to 300 sq. ft. It was fitted to No. 4011, *Knight of the Garter*.

A modification in 1908 resulted in Swindon No. 2 Superheater appearing. In this, as applied to No. 2922, *Saint Gabriel*, the diameter of the pipes was reduced to $1\frac{1}{4}$ in., giving a surface area of 275 sq. ft. As a result of experience gained, Swindon Superheater No. 3 was designed in 1909. In this, the field tube principle was abandoned in favour of one with three return bends per element, so that there were three parallel flows of steam up and back in each flue. The pipes adopted were 1 in. dia. and were fixed in a hollow steel casting of horseshoe shape, the fixing bolt to secure the element to the header being at the top of its bend. On each side of it were holes for communicating with the pockets in the header for supplying saturated steam and taking away the resulting superheated steam, so that one bolt served for both joints.

The legs of each casting had three holes in the back, one above the other, into which the pipes were fixed by expanding them in place, access being

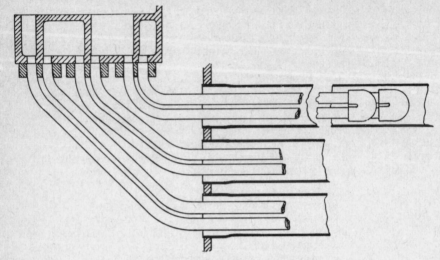

FIG. 43.   *The Schmidt superheater*

obtained in the front of the casting through holes which were afterwards closed by means of screwed taper plugs.   The height of the header was fixed so that it came midway between the upper and lower rows of flue tubes. The bottom row of elements had the legs downwards for the elements to enter the lower row of flue tubes and the top row of elements were reversed for entry into the upper row.   The header was honeycombed with passages for the entry and exit of steam, so arranged that, when the elements were bolted up, each made joint with the appropriate holes in the casting.

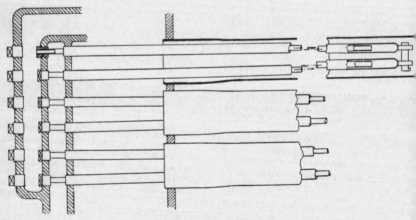

FIG. 44.   *The Cole superheater*

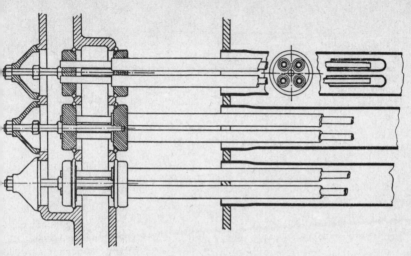

FIG. 45. *The Swindon No. 1 superheater*

No. 4021, then named *King Edward*, was the first to be fitted. It had 14 flue tubes of 5 in. dia. in two rows containing a total of 84 pipes of 1 in. dia., giving a surface of 260 sq. ft. A total of 84 pipes of 1 in. dia. was also used with the No. 4 boiler, but, owing to shorter length, the superheater surface was 191.8 sq. ft. For No. 2 boiler, only six flue tubes were provided, a single row, so that there were 36 pipes of 1 in. dia., giving a surface of 82.3 sq. ft.*

No. 3 Swindon Superheater became the standard and has remained so. The surface area was less than in the earlier types, as the aim was to raise the temperature of the steam no more than would ensure dry steam at exhaust, and this eased the cylinder lubrication problem. The high temperature of the Schmidt system was not favoured on this account. The mechanical lubricator as fitted to No. 2901 was rather regarded as a " box of tricks," and something simpler was sought. The first attempt was a force feed arrangement consisting of a cylinder which was fixed in a horizontal position on the platform above one of the cylinders. This was furnished with a ram with a tail rod screwed with a fine thread, which engaged a revolving nut held in thrust bearings and actuated by ratchet

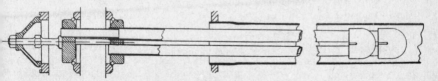

FIG. 46. *The Swindon No. 2 superheater*

*The No. 2 boiler up to 1916 had a double row superheater with six flue tubes in each row. This pattern had a heating surface of 153.5 sq. ft., later increased to 185sq. ft. The single row superheater with six flue tube was first applied to the No. 5 boiler in 1913

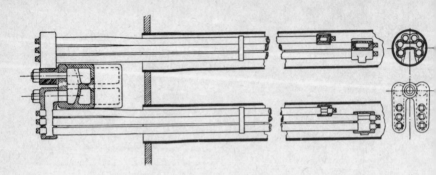

FIG. 47. *The Swindon No. 3 superheater*

wheel and pawl linked to the valve spindle. The slow rotation of the nut gradually forced the ram forward in the cylinder so that oil was displaced under pressure and distributed to pistons and valves. This arrangement was simple enough, but it was soon given up owing to the long and tedious process of refilling the container at sheds by screwing back the ram by hand.

With the lower steam temperature adopted, a new sight feed lubricator was designed, and the use of this has remained the practice with the No. 3 Superheater ever since. The earlier superheater headers were boxed in and fitted with a damper actuated by a servo-cylinder on the side of the smokebox. Admission of steam to the cylinder brought about the opening of the damper and counterweights closed it when the regulator was shut. This precaution against burning of the superheater return bends was found to be unnecessary and was given up with the No. 3 Superheater.

After the four-cylinder engines had been in service a little time and some experience gained, it was possible to compare them and the equivalent two-cylinder engines. The opinion expressed by the locomotive footplate inspectors was that the four-cylinder engines were " a coach better " with train loads of 12 to 14 or more vehicles at 60 m.p.h. and over. As they carried the same boiler, the superiority might be attributed in part to the valve gear, as it was inadvisable to notch up the Stephenson gear of the two-cylinder engines to less than 20 per cent., and partly to the better balancing of the four-cylinder arrangement resulting in lowered engine resistance. At lower speeds the two-cylinder engines had the advantage in acceleration due to the characteristics of their valve gear; parity between the two designs appeared to be in the region of 40 m.p.h.

This capability of all the two-cylinder types of giving high acceleration to trains from rest was limited at cut-offs of more than 40 per cent. by the disturbance caused to the fire by the explosive-like exhaust beats resulting from the use of long travel valves. Churchward thought that if a reservoir of some kind was interposed between the cylinders and blast pipe it would soften and prolong each exhaust beat. I was put on to find a way of carrying this out, and on examining the drawing of the cylinder and half saddle saw that the exhaust pipes passed through a box-like structure with vertical and horizontal walls, the wall which formed the base having large core holes of rectangular shape. These were large enough to allow access to the exhaust passages for the purpose of cutting away a part of the pipe.

The scheme was therefore to plate over the core holes after making large apertures in the pipes so that the exhaust steam could spill over into the chamber, so formed, at release and flow out with drop in pressure. The core holes were sealed, for the purpose of the experiment, by inserting endwise rectangular plates rather longer than the holes. These were turned over inside and bedded on to soft packing to form a joint, being pulled down by studs passing through bridges on the outside, after the manner of a mud-hole door. This extempore solution received commendation and instructions were given for an engine to be prepared for a test. This duly took place, but the report received nonplussed all, for the verdict was that the reservoirs had no appreciable effect on the exhaust beats.

Remembering that the Wolverhampton engines had at one time an exhaust relief valve below the cylinders, I brought this forward for review. This valve was of the butterfly type and was controlled from the footplate through rodding attached to its arm. By partly or fully opening the valve, the driver could discharge part of the exhaust under the engine and so moderate the blast. In re-applying this well-tried and reliable device, I proposed to locate the valve on the back of the blast pipe and carry a vent pipe from it to discharge steam behind the chimney, so by-passing some of the exhaust steam. The objection raised to it was that under the changed circumstances of the day it was no longer desirable to fit hand-operated devices. Experience in the past had shown that various apparatus fitted to sharpen or soften the blast was liable either to abuse or neglect, and something simple and automatic was required. Under the difficult conditions in the smokebox in the way of heat, dust and charred oil, anything involving sliding surfaces or springs to control valves under pressure was apt to get out of order quickly.

Someone put forward the suggestion of a dead-weight, directly-loaded valve as used on safety valves of stationary boilers; this line was pursued and it resulted in what became known as the " jumper top." The blast pipe was surrounded by a loose cylindrical casting having an upper lip machined to seat on the outside of the blast pipe orifice. Being of larger diameter than the top, the casting enclosed an annular chamber and this communicated with the exhaust through a number of holes set radially at some distance below the orifice. A circular projection from the blast pipe top closely fitted the ring near its base, so that steam could not escape downwards, but was free to lift the ring by pressure acting below the lip bearing on the seating. This upward lift was limited by stops. The device was tested in service and its weight adjusted until it ceased to function with cut-offs of less than 40 per cent. It then became a standard fitting. (Fig. 48).

What is remarkable is that no other railway has taken up the device*. Many years later when I was with the Southern Railway, a standard jumper

---

*The jumper top was fitted to some of Gresley's streamlined Pacifics on the L.N.E.R

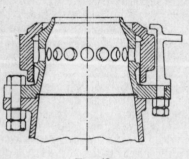

FIG. 48.
Jumper top for blastpipe

top was obtained from Swindon for trial. The engine on which it was fitted had many characteristics of G.W.R. design, the tapered Belpaire boiler with 200 lb. pressure, regulator in smokebox and cylinders with 10 in. dia. long travel valves and having short and direct ports in the cylinders, but it had Walschaerts valve gear. I made many trips with this engine before and after fitting, but could find no appreciable benefit resulting from the use of the jumper top. It is evident that G.W.R. engines possess characteristics no others have, no doubt partly due to the retardation of the steam admission point at the start and the gradual advance as cut-off is shortened, resulting from the Stephenson gear, whereas in those having gears with a fixed admission steam enters the cylinders before the end of the stroke and the piston is opposed. This is analogous to a motor car engine with automatic spark advance and retardation compared with one with a fixed spark at all speeds.

Again, the well-proportioned and positively lubricated regulator valve seems to give such control that drivers have confidence in opening up well at the start. Passengers riding near the front end of a Great Western train can feel every vigorous piston stroke transmitted through the drawgear during the period of high acceleration.

Due to the use of larger freight engines and consequent heavier loading of trains, great economies in operation were effected. Freight train mileage fell by 14 per cent. over the period 1900-08, while at the same time freight tonnage rose by 35 per cent. The motive power was provided by the 2-8-0s the " Aberdares," the 2-6-2 tanks, and for a time by the short-lived "Krugers." The principal routes to which this applied included Severn Tunnel Junction to London, the loads being made up to 65 of coal between Stoke Gifford and Swindon and up to 80 of coal between Swindon and London; and with 100 empties on return. Between Birmingham (Bordesley Junction) and London, maximum loads were 50 of coal to Banbury and 70 from Banbury to London, returning with 70 empties, for which service the " Aberdares " were used. On the Bristol to Plymouth section, loads were up to 80 goods wagons between Bristol and Exeter, with assistance of a bank engine over the Whiteball summit; between Taunton and Bristol 100 goods were taken. Other workings were between Aberdare and Salisbury, while on the Eastern and Western Valleys of Monmouthshire train loads down the valleys were made up to 70 of coal, with 70 empties on return; heavy iron ore trains were also worked. This shorter-distance haulage was done by the 2-6-2 tanks. The passage of heavy loads through the Severn Tunnel required the assistance of a pilot engine in front and the attachment of a second brake van in rear to ensure stretching of train to take up the slack in the loose couplings and so avoid snatches when passing from down to up gradient.

Services of express braked goods and perishable trains were introduced in 1905. The first of these to be run, apart from the existing established

No. 3311 *Bulldog* as re-boilered with a No. 2 standard boiler (originally numbered 3312). (93)

" Flower " Class engine No. 4118 *Polyanthus*. (122)

Single-wheeler No. 3027 *Worcester* with No. 2 boiler. (117)

109

De Glehn compound No. 102, *La France*. (86)

No. 181, 4-4-2 type. (94)

De Glehn compound No. 104 (later named *Alliance*). (93)

4-cylinder engine No. 40, *North Star*, 4-4-2 type. (94)

4-cylinder engine No. 4001, *Dog Star*, 4-6-0 type. (98)

" Saint " class engine No. 2916, *Saint Benedict*. (98)

4-cylinder engine No. 111, *The Great Bear*, 4-6-2 type. (120)

No. 97, Churchward's prototype 2-8-0 freight engine. (83)

No. 4700, 2-8-0 mixed traffic engine with No. 1 boiler. (137)

No. 4703, 2-8-0 mixed traffic engine with No. 7 boiler. (142)

" 4201 " class engine No. 4231, 2-8-0T. (133)

meat and fish trains, was that from Acton to Bristol and back. Other train services were started up as the number of brake-fitted vehicles put into traffic increased, covering all main lines and some cross-country routes. Trains were composed of 40 to 60 wagons, of which a minimum of 33 per cent. and a maximum of 35 wagons had to be fitted with the vacuum brake and coupled next to the locomotive. These had Instanter or screw couplings. This permitted average speeds of 35 m.p.h. and a maximum of 45 m.p.h.

As far as possible, the non-fitted wagons behind the vacuum head had oil axleboxes, but due to scarcity of these it was at first inevitable to include some wagons with grease boxes. As such boxes were liable to overheat at fast speed, it was necessary to halt these trains every 40 miles or so for a special examination to be made. In the course of time as more wagons with oil axleboxes were put into traffic, it became possible to eliminate wagons with grease boxes and so save time on the journey by cutting out stops, while average speeds were raised to 40 m.p.h. Passenger engines were used for working the trains, the "Bulldogs," for instance. The Birkenhead meat train, however, had been running for many years before 1905. It was composed of 30 to 40 vans and vacuum-braked throughout, the brake van being piped and fitted with a guard's van valve. It ran from Birkenhead to Oxley Sidings, 86 miles, and from Oxley Sidings to Acton, non-stop, 139 miles, whence it passed over the Metropolitan Railway to Smithfield market. This train was worked to Acton by a passenger engine.

The period 1903-08 was the heyday of the steam rail motor car. The vogue, which began about 1903, spread to many railways. The G.W.R. design comprised a coach body on underframe, mounted on two bogies. The trailing bogie was of standard carriage type, but the power bogie was of special design and a modification of the Dean suspension bogie; it carried a vertical multi-tubular boiler, which acted as the centre pin by the fitting of rubbing plates at front, back and sides to engage the members of the under-frame. Spring-backed pads were provided at the front and back running plates to take up slackness. Outside cylinders of 12 in. dia. by 16 in. stroke drove two pairs of coupled wheels of 8 ft. wheelbase. The balanced valve, with $1\frac{1}{8}$ in. lap and $4\frac{1}{2}$ in. maximum travel were controlled by Walschaerts valve gear. The coach body was of open saloon type with a driving com-partment at the trailing end, equipped with a regulator handle and rodding, brake valve, whistle and bell communication with the footplate, to enable the driver to control the car when running in reverse direction, the fireman remaining on the footplate.

A total of 99 cars was built, mostly at Swindon but a few from contrac-tors. The bodywork and interior arrangement was varied to suit the service, suburban, country branch or main line. The power units were in excess of the number of cars in order to provide spares for interchange, as they were all virtually alike except as regards wheel diameter, and there were no modifications of consequence after the first were made. The majority were built at Swindon, but a few were provided by Wolverhampton and contrac-tors. Coupled wheels were either 3 ft. $6\frac{1}{2}$ in. dia. or 4 ft. for faster running where conditions favoured that rather than rapid acceleration between frequent stops. The first two cars, built for service in the Stroud Valley, had 3 ft. 8 in. wheels. The weight of the complete power bogie with 4 ft. wheels was 8 tons, 9 cwt. without boiler.

These cars were well established before I moved to Swindon, so I had no part in them, but one small improvement which I was instrumental in getting made concerned the blast arrangement. Originally the exhaust piping was brought through the side of the smokebox and turned upwards, the end being swaged in to form a contracted orifice below the chimney, a somewhat crude arrangement. My sketch of a properly made and machined elbow casting with detachable cap was approved, and the fitting was applied as cars came to shops, to improve steaming. Maintenance was light except as regards the boiler, in which the tubes were difficult of access. If any work was required on it, the most satisfactory way was to lift the boiler out through the roof by crane and set it on the ground. The high centre of gravity of the boiler above frames set up racking strains in them and looseness of the rivets in the frames ensued unless the riveting was well done.

In service the cars ran well, though there was some boxing of the power bogie, especially when steam was shut off and in running downhill; 75 per cent. of the weight of the reciprocating parts was balanced. This horizontal rotative oscillation about the vertical centre line caused the suspension links to give rise to a vertical oscillation of the car body, but it was not sufficiently prolonged as to cause discomfort and was little felt at the rear of the car. Speed was about 30 m.p.h. on the average, with a maximum of 40 m.p.h., and acceleration was rapid; mileages were up to 220 per day. Where peaks of traffic demanded it, a trailer, or even two, would be taken if the profile of the line and timing of the service permitted. The cars were even used for shunting at remote stations and were known to draw seven or eight horseboxes or two to three coal wagons on occasion. The railcars gradually died out from 1914 onwards, but it was not until 1935 that the last was withdrawn in favour of the auto-train.

One disadvantage of railcars was the question of servicing in shed yards or repairs at sheds. The cars took up a lot of room and coaling had to be done by hand by emptying bags of coal into the bunker. Paintwork of the body was liable to be soiled by dust and smoke if brought amongst locomotives. It was here that engines of auto-trains had the advantage. Churchward proposed to try an intermediate arrangement by which the engine part of a car could be readily detached if any work was needed on the engine itself, something after the nature of a pony and trap, in which the " trap " could be parked in a siding while the " pony " was released from the shafts to go to " stable." I was put on to develop the scheme, but we could not produce anything very practicable so the idea was dropped.

The steam railcars died out when road transport in the shape of motor-buses in rural areas drew off traffic; in other cases the cars created so much traffic that they had to be replaced by auto-trains. To meet the demand in more populous areas, auto-trains were introduced in 1905. In these a small tank engine of normal design pulled or propelled two coaches. The outer end of one coach was fitted up as a driving compartment, as in the railcars, and the coaches and locomotive carried rodding with universal joints at couplings, so that the regulator on the locomotive could be operated from the remote end, with the locomotive propelling; bell communication was provided, as on the railcars.

The tank engines were usually the Wolverhampton " 517 " class, of 0-4-2 type with 5 ft. 2 in. wheels, or " 2021 " class, 0-6-0 type with 4 ft. 1½ in. wheels, depending on circumstances as to route and service. These tank engines were of adequate power and so could take two additional coaches at peak periods, but it was thought undesirable that the locomotive should propel four coaches from the rear and so the practice was to have two in front and two behind. The appearance of a fussy little tank engine in the middle of the train caused apprehension to some nervous passengers and so it was decided to make its presence less conspicuous by enclosing the whole locomotive in a housing to match the coach body, both in profile and colour.

The design of this " dressing of the wolf in sheep's clothing " consisted of a casing of thin steel plates for top and sides, curved to coach profile, there being unglazed openings in place of windows for ventilation. The sides were painted to match the cream and umber colour of the trailers. It was much in the style of the steam tramway locomotives formerly seen in the streets of industrial areas in the latter days of the Victorian Era, and was provided for much the same reason. The dressing of locomotives in this style was not to the liking of the running department, as it affected availability for other duties, and it was given up in 1911 and the locomotives had enclosed cabs as a substitute. The auto-train will, no doubt, give way in time to diesel-driven multiple units.

Superheating brought to a head the need for improvements in lubrication of cylinders and valves. In earlier days a tallow pot with spout was always to be found on a tray fixed above the firehole door, by which location the grease was kept in liquid form and could be poured into the simple open or closed cup lubricators at the cylinders, or used to fill a small closed cylindrical vessel situated behind the chimney and feeding into the regulator box, whence the lubricant was carried with the flow of steam to the steam chest and cylinders. With saturated steam of not more than 150 lb. per sq. in. pressure distributed by slide valves, little lubricant was required and the simple devices sufficed. About 1893 a change-over from tallow to mineral oil compounded with a small percentage of rape oil occurred, and for this displacement type lubricators were adopted. The closed lubricator had a needle valve for regulation of the feed, and steam which found its way into the lubricator condensed and the water so formed gradually lifted the oil, so that it seeped out into the steam supply to the cylinders.

This sufficed when stops were made at intervals of 50 miles or so and there was an opportunity to refill, if necessary, at station stops. When longer non-stop runs began in 1895, the lubricator had to be enlarged and brought into the cab so that it was immediately under the control of the driver for regulation, and, if necessary, for refilling en route. Oil was conveyed to the front end by a long pipe under the lagging. There was, however, no indication of the rate of feed, and the amount of opening of the needle valve had to be found from experience.

This lubricator was superseded by one with sight feed, there being two short glass tubes enclosing oil nipples. The glasses were kept full of water

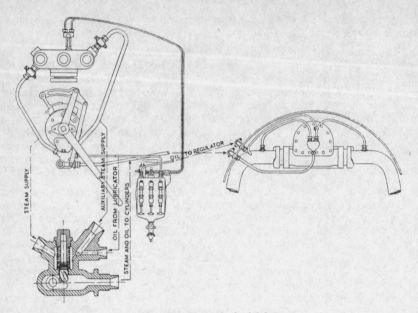

FIG. 49.   *Swindon sight-feed lubricator*

so that drops of oil issuing from the nipples could be seen as they rose in the water, and thereby the supply could be regulated to a nicety.   Only one glass was in use at a time; the other was a spare in case of breakage of the glass in service or in the event of blockage, the changeover being made through a two-way cock.   A condenser coil under the cab roof ensured a sufficient head of water to elevate the oil to the level of the regulator box. The delivery was made by a pipe carried under the lagging for warmth.   The triple sight-feed lubricator was developed from this about 1908.   One feed went to the regulator box as before, but a second supply was carried along in a larger pipe by a current of steam to a junction box inside the smokebox. From this, two branches divided the supply and carried it to the upper part of each of the main steam pipes, whence it flowed in pulverised form to the steam chests and cylinders.   One sight-feed glass for cylinders was used at a time, with the other spare, as before.   According to my calculation book, the capacity of the lubricator was 7.8 pints.   When superheating was established, the same arrangement was used, but the lubricant was introduced into the two main steam pipes below the superheater header.   (Fig. 49).

The early and experimental superheaters aimed at steam temperatures of about 650°F., and this led to much decomposition of the oil, and the mechanical lubricators tried failed to spread the lubricant sufficiently at the points of local application.   By lowering steam temperature to about 500°F. and feeding the oil through sight-feed lubricators with an admixture of saturated steam, much better conditons existed for efficient lubrication. This applied as long as the regulator was open, but in drifting any distance with the regulator shut conditions were not so good in the piston valve engines, as the pumping action of the cylinders drew in smokebox gases and dust to dry and contaminate the surfaces. Two or three years later the difficulty was overcome by the addition of a combining valve in a box fixed below the regulator stuffing box in the cab. This contained a spring-loaded mushroom valve, lifted by an internal cam through an external arm and shaft. The arm was connected to the free end of a hinged quadrant plate fixed above the regulator stuffing box. The regulator rod had a short arm carrying a pin to engage with the quadrant. In the raised position the slot of the quadrant was radial to the regulator rod and, therefore, remained in a set position. The end of the slot being inclined at an angle upwards resulted in the pin lowering the quadrant end and connecting link and so dropping the combining valve on its seat and cutting off communication between the lubricator and cylinders, since the delivery had to pass by way of the combining valve box. (Fig. 49).

Besides the main supply of steam to the combining valve box, there was an auxiliary supply through another pipe entering at a different point. This picked up the lubricant as delivered and carried it on to meet the main supply, coming by way of the combining valve, after passing through a restricted orifice. By this simple means the auxiliary supply pipe was under constant boiler pressure, but the oil could enter it under the additional head given by the column of water supplied by the lubricator condenser. The setting up of an artificial back pressure by means of the orifice assured a constancy of oil supply under variation of steam chest pressure or its absence. After closing the regulator valve in the smokebox while running, the regulator handle was moved back to a bullet stop, at which point the jockey valve of the regulator had not moved sufficiently to re-open to steam, but the quadrant plate had, under the small angular movement, re-opened the combining valve so that the lubricant and a limited supply of saturated steam were passing to the main steam pipes in the smokebox. Therefore, while the engine was running with the regulator closed, the steam chests and cylinders were filled with oily steam vapour, so largely excluding the smokebox gases from entering by way of the blast pipe. The supply of steam was insufficient to create any drawbar pull, and the regulator handle was only moved to its fully closed position as the train neared a stop.

About 1907, difficulty was being found in selecting suitable turns of duty for the whole of the 80 single-wheelers of the " 3001 " class. Churchward seemed reluctant to let them go and sought to improve their performance beyond giving them domeless Belpaire boilers. These had to be of the older "Camel" pattern with cylindrical barrel, as the tapered boiler barrels would not fit between the wheels at normal height of boiler. Apart from that, I was put on to see whether long-travel valves could be introduced; the steam lap was already $1\frac{1}{8}$ in. and to increase it to, say, $1\frac{5}{8}$ in. necessitated a good deal more valve travel. As the motion was direct, and not through rocking levers, this could be done only by using larger eccentrics, but the limited clearances at various points made the scheme impracticable.

A little later on Churchward came along with the idea of converting the single-wheelers into 4-4-0 type in line with the " Armstrong " class, by substituting two pairs of 7 ft. 2 in. coupled wheels in place of the existing driving and trailing carrying wheels. The diameter of the single wheels was at that time 7 ft. 9 in. due to the use of thicker tyres. The difference was therefore 7 inches, and he said he was prepared to see the cylinder centre line pass 3½ in. above the driving centre, as against 2½ in. in his standard engines. This would leave the engine at the same height above rails. I got out a scheme on these lines, extending the driving horns downwards and adding a patch to the frames at the trailing end to take trailing coupled wheels. The snags in this scheme were that due to the lowering of the driving centre there was lack of clearance between connecting rods and bottom slide bars and the valve gear was deranged as a whole. An alternative scheme was to lower the whole engine 3½ inches, but this necessitated smaller bogie wheels and a raising of buffer beam and drag box, thus adding to the cost of conversion. Churchward did not think the expense was justified, so he reluctantly agreed to the older ones of the class being scrapped as they completed their mileage. Some were withdrawn in 1908, but it was not until 1916 that the last one went, No. 3074, which had been stationed at Taunton and was condemned in December, 1915.

The last of the 2-2-2 single-wheelers survived almost as long, for the remaining two, Nos. 1128 and 165, which finished their days on the Fairford branch, were withdrawn in April, 1914 and January, 1915, respectively. With the passing of the single-wheelers, something was lost in the finer points of driving. Any ham-handed man could take on a coupled engine with the loads prevailing at the time, but it required great skill, delicacy of touch and long experience to get away with a train from rest, where adhesion was limited to that provided by a single pair of wheels, 20 tons being the maximum axleload at the turn of the century. A little slipping of the wheels at starting was to be expected and usually occurred, but it was just a quiet spinning from time to time and was quickly checked. As soon as the train was well on the move this tendency stopped and the single-wheeler then had the advantage over its coupled equivalent in smooth running and more economical coal consumption, other than in exceptional weather conditions where the rails were greasy generally and there might be a little loss of time on gradients, due to more prolonged slipping.

One recalls the feat of No. 3065, *Duke of Connaught* in 1904, when it took a special Ocean Mail train from Bristol to Paddington in under 100 minutes, despite a severe check to walking pace, due to a speed restriction necessitated by repairs to the Cricklade Road Bridge at Swindon. From that point an average speed of 80 m.p.h. was maintained over the next 70 miles to London. On a fine early Autumn day, about 1909, on seeing a single-wheeler passing through Swindon with what seemed to be an interminably long train, I stopped to count the coaches. There were no fewer than 23 eight-wheelers, mostly corridor stock, and the tare weight would be in excess of 500 tons. This was empty stock being worked back mid-week from West London Sidings to the West of England to bring back the returning holiday-makers. Beyond two short stretches of 1 in 660 between Didcot and Swindon, the engine encountered only easy gradients and so was able to jog along at 35 m.p.h. or so, once it had the great mass of train on the move. Dean's 7 ft. 8 in. single-wheelers were regarded by many as the most beautiful engines ever built anywhere. Many more still would agree with that if it applied to the products of Swindon only.

The brake gear on the standard bogie was a source of trouble to the running department, owing to the necessity for frequent adjustment to keep it effective. As the brake cylinder was only 11 in. in diameter, the leverage had to be large to produce sufficient pressure on the brake blocks; the whole of the stroke of the cylinder was taken up with ¼ in. clearance and ¼ in. wear of blocks.

This problem was turned over to me for investigation, and I was able to work in a 13 in. cylinder, thereby reducing the leverage and permitting 40 per cent. more block wear before adjustment became necessary. At the same time I was able to introduce improvements in the detail design of the cylinder, and afterwards carried these improvements into the whole range of engine brake cylinders, 18 in., 22 in., 26 in. and 30 in., by re-designing them.

In 1908 the connecting links were completed to form a line from Birmingham to Cheltenham. The principal new work was a new line from Tyseley, south of Birmingham, to Stratford-on-Avon. An up-to-date engine shed at Tyseley superseded the old Bordesley shed, which dated from broad-gauge days. For the new services which then began from Wolverhampton and Birmingham to Cardiff, Bristol, and the West, the new " Flower " class were used. A new terminal station was built at Moor Street, Birmingham, for suburban trains from the south of the city. This was remarkable in having traverser tables at the buffer stops so that the locomotive could be released on the adjacent road without having to remove the train. This station was provided to relieve Snow Hill Station of some of the local passenger services and avoid their passing through the bottleneck of the approach tunnel.

Another cross-country route inaugurated was from Cardiff to Yarmouth and Lowestoft. New connections put in at Leamington enabled through trains to run via Honeybourne, Leamington, Rugby and Peterborough. The L.N.W.R. engines took over at Leamington and handed over to the G.E.R. at Peterborough. Water troughs laid in near Lostwithiel enabled non-stop runs to be made from Plymouth to Penzance.

In the same year the Port Talbot Railway and the South Wales Mineral Railway were taken over by the G.W.R. I was sent to Port Talbot to measure up the under-clearances of some of their tank engines to make sure that they would clear the girders of the Severn Bridge, as it was planned to bring them to Swindon over the old Severn & Wye line to re-boiler with a Swindon domeless Belpaire boiler.* Also from this time the very useful standard 2-6-2 tanks were increased in power by fitting them with the No. 4 boiler in place of the No. 2, commencing with No. 3150.

The building of the first and only example of the " Pacific " type on the G.W.R. took place in 1908. Basically it was the " Star " class as far as frames, cylinders, wheels, motion and bogie were concerned. Extension frames in the form of slabs, and a radial axle for carrying wheels were added at the trailing end, so producing the 4-6-2 type. This was No. 111, *The Great Bear*.

The principal feature of this design was the large boiler, designated

*These two engines, P.T.R. Nos. 20 and 21, 0-8-2 tank type, were of American make with bar frames. The new boilers were made up of Standard 1 Boiler pressed plates

No. 6, with wide Belpaire firebox. The barrel, 23 ft. long by 5 ft. 6 in. dia. at smokebox and 6 ft. at firebox, was made up of three rings, the first and third parallel and the second coned, but with its axis horizontal. The firebox, which had a sloping back plate, was 8 ft. long by 6 ft. 6 in. wide at front and 5 ft. 9 in. at back and had the front leg set forward, but there was no combustion chamber, as experience of it with the " Kruger " class has not proved satisfactory. The grate had 41.8 sq. ft. of area, with the back half horizontal and the front section inclined. Originally, the brick arch was carried on four 3 in. bore water tubes, but these were not replaced after they burnt out. The heating surface of the boiler tubes was 2,673 sq. ft. and that of the firebox 158 sq. ft., a total of 2,831 sq. ft. The Swindon No. 1 superheater fitted had 545 sq. ft. of area and the boiler pressure was 225 lb. per sq. in. Churchward thought that a standard six-wheeled tender would look insignificant behind so large a locomotive, so he had a special bogie tender made. This had a flat-bottom tank and the two bogies were of the standard locomotive pattern of bar-frame construction; the wheelbase was reduced to 5 ft. 9 in. and side play was omitted, but bolsters with side-bearing blocks were added.

My part in the design was to produce the cylinders, but very little latitude was permitted, for Churchward insisted on the general layout of the " Star " class cylinders and motion being followed and the cylinders enlarged only as much as the circumstances would allow. The trailing bogie wheel came behind the outside cylinder and there was very little clearance to permit side play and angular movement of the wheel, taking into consideration that the total wheelbase of the engine was greater than in the 4-6-0 type and therefore the throwover would be greater. Clearance of the leading bogie wheel and the inside cylinder also had to be watched, so a bore of 15 in. was as far as it was practical to go. The Great Western locomotive tyres were 5¾ in. wide, whereas on the other railways a width of 5½ in. or even 5¼ in. was common, and I pointed out that if narrower tyres were used it would be possible to increase the bore beyond 15 in. Churchward would not agree to that and seemed to be quite content to leave it at 15 in.

It could be inferred from this that the large boiler with wide firebox and large grate area in conjunction with relatively small cylinders was a reversion to the broad-gauge practice of having a large reserve of boiler power. The " Star " class could handle the longest trains that the Paddington platforms would accommodate at that time, and therefore more tractive effort through larger cylinders was not really called for. The big boiler would, however, enable higher average speed to be attained through faster running on up gradients, due to the reserve of power. In accordance with the policy of braking all wheels, blocks were required for the trailing radial truck, and I was called on to produce a scheme. As the box had 4½ in. side play each way and the blocks had to follow, use of the ordinary fixed brake hanger was out of the question, nor could any attachment be made to the sliding box. The problem had therefore to be solved on original lines. After an acceptable brake gear operated by a separate 18 in. vacuum cylinder had been produced it was worked into the general arrangement, but it came as a disappointment when the plan had to be jettisoned because the back end of the engine was coming out too heavy.

The appearance of *The Great Bear* brought much prestige to the G.W.R. and the resulting publicity was a great asset. In service, however, the engine did nothing very remarkable. Its axle load of 20 tons 9 cwt. per coupled axle* restricted its running to the operation of passenger and brake-fitted freight trains between London and Bristol only. The radial truck proved to be the " Achilles heel," for it frequently overheated. Side thrust on this box had to be taken up by the back of the wheel boss on each side, and as this was a point difficult to lubricate efficiently and the surfaces were in a position where ashpan dust and grit thrown up in the four-foot could reach them, the boxes were liable to overheat on the least provocation.

I came upon the same sort of thing many years later, on the Southern Railway when riding with " King Arthur " class engines. Some of these had Drummond bogie tenders in which the axleboxes were on the inside of the wheels while others had the Urie bogie tender with outside bearings. The boxes of the former invariably ran at " blood heat," whereas the latter ran almost cold, due to better thrust conditions and being in a position where air cooling was more effective. If, instead of tenaciously clinging to a radial axlebox common to several classes, *The Great Bear* had been fitted with the modern type of radial truck with outside bearings, more might have been heard of the engine. It was also handicapped by the great length of the boiler barrel, as in the absence of a combustion chamber the tubes were unduly long in relation to their diameter and so steaming was not as free as it should have been.

It is often asked: " Why was *The Great Bear* built?" No official reason has ever been stated, but it seems probable that the fine performance of the " Star " class prompted the directors to seek to raise the running standards even higher, and they called upon Churchward to see what could be done in the matter. With an eye to future development, the Chief Civil Engineer had for some years been replacing the older bridges by new construction capable of taking axle loadings of 22½ tons. This had been completed only on the London-Bristol section, though the renewals were being made elsewhere with stronger bridges as a matter of routine, but this was a long-term affair and could not be completed for a number of years.

Under the very restricted route availability at the time, *The Great Bear* became a " white elephant " to the running department, for it was difficult to fit it into more than a few set jobs. It is said of Churchward that when he was told of the appearance of H. N. Gresley's Pacific on the Great Northern Railway in 1922, he remarked: " What did that young man want to *build* one for: we could have *sold* him ours." Two years later, after Churchward's retirement, *The Great Bear* was converted into the 4-6-0 type, in September, 1924, as its boiler required very heavy repairs.

Contemporary with the building of *The Great Bear* came 20 more 2-6-2 tanks of the " 3150 " series, together with 10 more of the small 2-6-2 tanks, first built at Wolverhampton, where they were known as Class " N3," Nos. 2181-90. Then there were 10 more 4-4-2 " County " tanks and another 10 " Stars," for which I had to re-design the outside slidebars.

In the midst of all this building of standard classes, it came somewhat as

---

*The official diagram gives the axle load as 20 tons, but a number of re-adjustments were made after the engine was in service. In " The British Steam Locomotive, 1825-1925 ", E. L. Ahrons quotes 20.45 tons.

a surprise that 20 of the double-framed 4-4-0 type " Atbara " class were to be built. These were known as the " Flower " class. They had No. 2 Boilers so that the axle loads would permit of working on the more restricted routes. It was explained to me later that Churchward was concentrating on furnishing the main lines with suitable locomotive power and that he had not yet made up his mind as to what he would do for the secondary services. The double-framed engines were being built as a stop-gap measure. This batch was, however, fitted with the vacuum brake in place of steam, and screw reversing gear instead of steam-operated.

My part in the " Flower " class was to re-design the Dean suspension bogie by converting it into the side bearing type, as used on the French engines. This was done by fixing ball brackets to the main frames and brackets with flat top surface to the bogie frames on which the intermediate cups were to slide. With the removal of the suspension links, the cross beams were shortened, and side control was provided at the centre pin through a pair of helical springs. (Fig. 50). After these came 15 double-framed engines of the 5 ft. 8 in. " Bulldog " class. These also had the new bogie, and were known as the " Bird " class.

In August, 1907, one of the French compounds, No. 104, was reboilered with a Swindon No. 1 boiler without superheater. For record purposes I was engaged in making an outline diagram of the engine by taking particulars of what had been done in the shops. Having occasion to open the smokebox door, I was confronted with a maze of pipes of various sizes, not only high- and low-pressure steam pipes, but above all the blast pipe was festooned with ejector exhaust and blower pipes whose ends had been bent by the coppersmiths into ring shape and drilled with a number of holes for

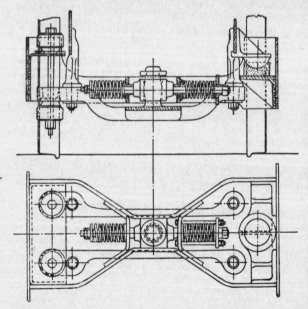

FIG. 50

The Dean bogie. Left half shows suspension type ; right half conversion to sliding type the emission of steam.   They were placed around the blast pipe orifice and clamped with hook bolts, a crude and clumsy arrangement, while the pipes leading to the position offered further obstruction for access to the tube plate.

The cast-iron chimney, as used in the " Atbara " and other classes, was in two portions, one the exterior chimney with short internal projection and the other the bell attached to it.   This included annular blower and ejector exhaust passages at the choke, so that the pipe connections were in the upper part of the smokebox and thus caused no obstruction.   When steel chimneys were adopted in the later designs, the coiled pipes, as on No. 104, were brought to the top of the blast pipe.   In order to restore the advantages of the earlier arrangement, I set about getting out a sketch of a cast-iron ring to be sandwiched between the base of the inner steel chimney and the steel bell, attachment being made by bolts through recessed flanges, top and bottom.   The annulus for the blower was below the ejector exhaust and it was drilled with a number of small holes at an inclination of 1 in 5, the jets from which met in the centre of the chimney.   While this form of blower uses rather more steam for a given draught, it has the great advantage of permitting work to be done in the smokebox when fire is on the grate.   The annulus for the ejector exhaust had a number of larger holes also at an inclination to the centre line.

When I brought this scheme forward, it was taken up with alacrity, and a pattern was made at once and a finished casting brought up for inspection. As a result, the bolting flanges were replaced by ears for the bolt holes and shallow recesses left to register the steel plates top and bottom, in order to lighten the casting.   With this one alteration, the " blower ring," as it was designated, was brought into production and made a standard fitting in several internal diameters to suit the various chimney sizes.   It was also taken up by other railways later on.   When Professor Goss published the results of his investigations into blast pipe and chimney proportions made on the Purdue Plant in the U.S.A., he set out the optimum proportions by means of empirical formulae.   A copy of these results was handed to me and I was instructed to apply them to the smokeboxes of the standard boilers, Nos. 1 to 5.   It did not take long to discover that the formulae were not wholly applicable to English conditions, owing to smaller smokebox diameters and chimneys restricted in height by loading gauge.   Therefore I was told to make the best compromise possible as a basis, with a view to chimneys and blast pipes being put into service and adjusted by experiment to find the best results.   When these were attained, I completed the dimensions of the standard smokeboxes, and all future ones were made to them, and existing ones brought into line as they passed through shops.   Later on, empirical formulae based on Swindon experience were produced to supersede those of Goss.

The Great Western relied almost entirely on the dynamometer car for testing of locomotives, and little or no use was made of the stationary plant for that purpose.   During my short time with the Testing Section, I had to give a hand by going through the long rolls of paper bearing the record of the test runs.   This was done by exposing one length after another of each roll and calibrating the lines with scales from datum lines and the serrations made by the time pen, and other data.   Search was made for outstanding

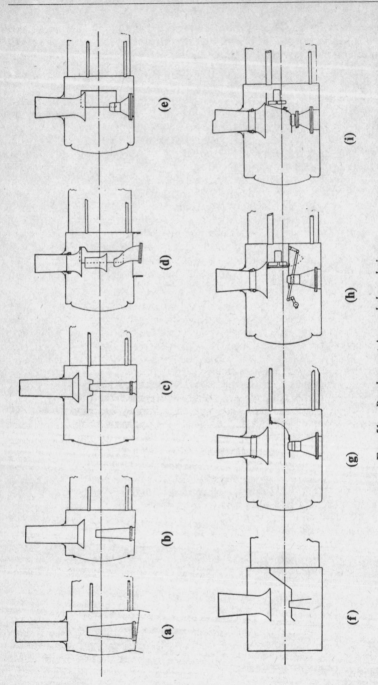

Fig. 51.   Development in smokebox design

(a) Armstrong: high blast pipe and parallel chimney.   (b) early Dean: chimney and blast pipe lowered due to higher boiler centre, chimney tapered inwards.   (c) "Duke of Cornwall" with diaphragm.   (d) "Atbara," with deflector plate.   (e) early Churchward with deflector plate.   (f) do. with diaphragm.   (g) according to Goss.   (h) superheater with damper gear added.   (i) final arrangement with jumper top and damper gear removed points in performance, which were marked on the roll and corrected for acceleration, plus or minus. These points were listed and, later, spotted on graphs in a record book with various coloured inks. Drawbar pull was plotted against speed and there were a number of hyperbolic lines of drawbar-horsepower, so that it was possible to see at a glance the highest performances of individual engines. This book was kept under lock and key as a " top priority " secret and anyone divulging its contents would be " shot at dawn " in those days. In entering up some of the points, I had the oppor-unity to make mental note of the records existing up to the time, and memory recalls that the highest drawbar-horsepower noted was that of a French compound with the Swindon No. 1 Superheater boiler. It was, however, obtained in the region of 40 or 45 m.p.h. and there were no points to indicate that it was any better than the Swindon engines at the higher piston speeds.

A proposal which I put forward for cylinder drain cocks was tried out on one of the Atlantics. In this the three plug cocks per cylinder were replaced by a single triple-ported cock. It simplified the operating gear and there was only one discharge pipe. When steam was shut off, the valve automatically opened to drain the cylinders and steam chests. After it had been running for a little time, I noticed a small blow of steam from the cock as the engine passed through Swindon, and this gradually got worse. Appar-ently the special cock was then taken off at one of the sheds and sent to the Works for attention, being replaced by the normal three-cock arrangement. Unfortunately the job was not followed up as it should have been, as no more was heard of it.

While I was with the boiler gang for a short time in 1909, Churchward came along and wanted to try the effect of increasing the water space of the firebox in the standard boilers from $3\frac{1}{2}$ in. to $4\frac{1}{2}$ in. The copper plates were, however, to be joggled above the foundation ring of normal width. This necessitated some alteration to the curvature of the upper part of the box on the sides, as also the wrapper plate. I had to make a number of attempts with the reversed curvatures in cross section before producing one which pleased Churchward's eye. After that he insisted that the end row of side stays and roof stays should not be brought too close to the lap in the plates. The firebox tube plate, in particular, must be allowed room to " breathe," he said. The alteration caused an increase in tube area and a decrease in firebox surface. In the case of the No. 2 boiler with 12 flue tubes, total heating surface inclusive of superheater was raised from 1182.9 to 1200.2 sq. ft.

The working of heavy coal trains in the Welsh valleys called for some modifications of the vacuum brake apparatus as at first fitted to the standard locomotives. The gradients were in favour of the loaded trains moving down to the ports, and so braking rather than tractive effort was called for in their movement. On the up journey tractive effort had to be exerted to haul the empties against the gradient. While engines with a steam brake were used there was no difficulty, as this was direct acting and speed could be regulated by the on and off movement of the handle in the absence of graduation of pressure by automatic means, as in some other types of brake valves.

With the vacuum brake, any air admitted to the train pipe to set the brakes was exhausted again by the action of the vacuum pump as soon as the application valve was shut. If left open a small amount to maintain a fixed reduction of vacuum, overheating of the pump was liable to occur on account of the increased volume under compression for discharge to atmosphere. At the same time, a prolonged period of braking would not permit of maintenance of full vacuum on the chamber, or reservoir, side of the brake piston against leakage. Some of the "3111" class of 2-6-2 tanks were fitted with small ejectors in place of pumps and, while these could be shut off during braking periods, they did not then maintain the reservoir vacuum. Also, when operating passenger trains, an excessive amount of steam was needed to maintain 25 in. of vacuum as compared with that for maintaining 20 in., the normal amount when ejectors are used.

This problem was put to me for solution by mechanical means, and the proposal which I started on had a changeover valve fixed beside the driver's brake valve and operated from a link from the application handle. The branch pipe from the pump was brought to the footplate so that the movement of the handle could switch the pump from train pipe to reservoir during braking. The difficulty here was to arrange for a "lap" position in which the admission valve was closed while the pump was in communication with the reservoir, without making alteration to the standard brake ejector. Simultaneously, someone else was endeavouring to solve the same problem by automatic means, and this offered more promise as a solution, as the switch-over of the pump from train pipe to reservoir could be arranged independently of the driver's application valve on the footplate. This scheme was therefore the one to be more fully developed.

The automatic valve finally introduced was known as the "retaining valve." It contained one moving part, a piston and a piston valve connected by a hollow stem. The valve casting had a cylinder formed in the top portion and the piston valve chamber below had three connections, one to reservoir below, to pump at the side and to train pipe opposite but at a higher level. In running, the valve was retained by its own weight on a seating at the reservoir connection. Above the piston valve the pump was in communication with the train pipe branch. Through the hollow stem the reservoir communicated with the cylinder above the piston, so that when a brake application was made, air admitted to the train pipe acted below the piston and raised it and the piston valve sufficiently to bring the pump in communication with the reservoir and cut it off from the train pipe. As regards the brake cylinder on the locomotive, the upward travel of the piston compressed the residual air in the upper part of the cylinder and in the reservoir, so that the vacuum therein was reduced from 25 in. to about 23 in., depending on the amount of travel resulting from the degree of wear of the brake blocks. In order that the pump could not create more than 23 in. while cut off from the train pipe, a second limit valve, or "pepper box," was added to the retaining valve to prevent this, otherwise the pump would produce the 25 in. for which its own limit valve was set.

On tender engines, a hose connection between engine and tender enabled the reservoir on the tender to be coupled by piping to that on the engine, non-return valves being added so that reservoir vacuum was not destroyed, with consequent loss of brake power, if engine and tender hoses were pulled apart through fracture of the drawbar. At a later date the retaining valve was modified by being inverted and having its pipe connections altered, but the principle of operation remained the same. The retaining valve became a standard fitting on vacuum-braked engines.

Steel water space side stays were introduced in 1909. Six horizontal rows of copper stays remained at the top of the box and one vertical row each side, front and back. The remainder were replaced by stays made from a special reeled steel, $\frac{5}{8}$ in. in dia. screwed into the plates and rotary caulked with a special hammer instead of being riveted over. Only a small projection was left on the outside of the box, but on the inside the projecting thread was long enough to carry a nut. This was expendable and its purpose was to protect the stay end from the fire, nuts being renewed at intervals as they burnt away. The nominal pitch of these stays was $3\frac{1}{2}$ in. compared with 4 in. for copper stays. Steel stays were renewed as required by larger sizes up to $\frac{3}{4}$ in. Above that size $\frac{7}{8}$ in. dia. steel stays were used and their ends were riveted over, as with copper stays.

In the summer of 1909, I obtained leave of absence to join a party of young engineers visiting Eastern Canada and the U.S.A. Border to see engineering works of various kinds. My object was to obtain first-hand knowledge of railways and locomotives there, both steam and electric. In accomplishing this, I gained some useful experience of locomotives in general, but what struck me as much as anything was the use made of the 2-6-0 freight engine with coupled wheels of 4 ft. 10 in. or 5 ft. dia. as a general purpose locomotive on secondary services and country branch lines. This was particularly in evidence on a long extension to the silver mines in Northern Ontario. Here all services, passenger, freight and shunting, were performed by the 2-6-0, so offering the maximum of availability, the greatest use from each unit and the minimum stock of spare parts in stores. Although dining cars and Pullmans were included in the passenger trains, speeds were very moderate in view of the small diameter of the coupled wheels, seldom exceeding 45 m.p.h. It struck me forcibly at the time that, given wheels of some 10 or 12 in. larger, such an engine could perform very useful work on English railways, where average speeds were about 10 m.p.h. higher.

On my return to Swindon in the autumn, I was asked to draw up a short report calling attention to anything seen which might be of benefit to the Great Western, and amongst other things I mentioned this extensive use of the 2-6-0 and its suitability to English conditions, given larger wheels. Shortly after, a roll of musty old drawings was deposited at my board. They related to some small 0-6-0 saddle tanks with outside cylinders and the Allan straight link valve motion, taken over from the former Cornwall Minerals Railway many years ago. These useful and indispensable little engines would go anywhere a wagon could, on account of their short wheelbase, such as curves at docks and wharves too sharp for the ordinary locomotives used for shunting. As the Cornish engines were getting old, they would need to be replaced by others of similar design, for no other class existed on the G.W. which could undertake their duties. The instructions were that I was to produce, single-handed, a complete new set of drawings,

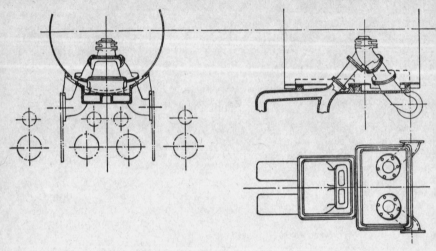

FIG. 52. *"Star" class exhaust arrangement*, 1905-10

adhering to existing patterns and templates for these engines, but outside that bringing every detail into line with current Swindon practices, and to suitably modify cab, bunkers, etc.; it would be a useful experience for me, I was told. Resulting from this was the building of five engines, Nos. 1361-5, in 1910.

Another task given me about this time was the re-design of the front end

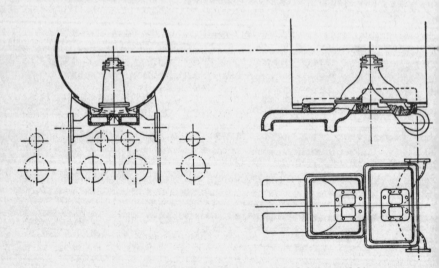

FIG. 53. *"Star" class exhaust arrangement with bifurcated blastpipe*

" 3100 " class engine No. 3104, 2-6-2T with 5 ft. 3 in. coupled wheels. (157)

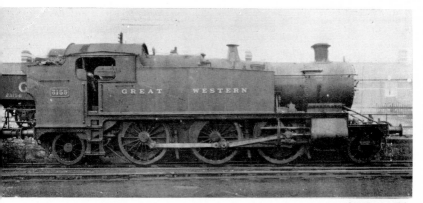

" 3150 " class engine No. 3155, 2-6-2T with 5 ft. 8 in. coupled wheels. (122)

" 8100 " class engine No. 8106, 2-6-2T with 5 ft. 6 in. coupled wheels. (156)

2-6-2T with 5 ft. 8 in
coupled wheels
Outside steam pipe
to cylinders. (147
[*A. A. Delicat*

Left: "4800" class
(renumbered 14000
engine No. 4817
0-4-2T. (148)
[*P. Ransome-Wall*

Below: "5600" class
engine No. 5636
0-6-2T for South
Wales. (141)

Right: No. 1361 0-6-0 Saddle Tank with outside cylinders. (127)
P. Ransome-Wallis

Below: "5400" class engine No. 5415, 0-6-0 Pannier Tank with 5 ft. 2 in. wheels. (148)
[Brian E. Morrison

Right: "5700" class engine No. 6707, 0-6-0 Pannier Tank with 4 ft. 7½ in. wheels. (148)
[R. C. Riley

131

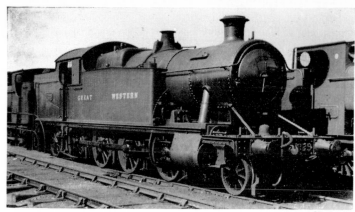

" 7200 " class engine No. 7229.   Originally a " 4200 " class 2-8-0T rebuilt as a 2-8-2T. (156)

" 4301 " class engine No. 4304 for mixed traffic. (135)

" 2251 " class freight engine No. 2254. (147)

of the " Star " class. The blast pipe was supported on three exhaust pipes coming up at an angle, like a three-legged stool. Not only was it difficult to set but the back legs formed some obstruction in getting to the tube plate. By alterations to the exhaust passages in the two saddles and the use of a bifurcated blast pipe spanning the two saddles, a more straightforward arrangement and streamlined effect resulted, and access to the tube plate was facilitated. Another new design appeared in 1910, a 2-8-0 type tank engine, No. 4201. It was virtually a tank engine version of the 2-8-0 standard freight engine, but, on account of the sharper curves of 6 ch. radius it would have to traverse, some side play in the trailing coupled wheels was necessary. Due to the close centres of the wheels, the components of the coupling rods were likewise short and this necessitated joints in the rod for both vertical and horizontal movements of the trailing wheels. My part in the design of this engine was to produce the coupling rods, and the problem of the dual movement was solved by a joint with spherical surfaces which could allow the rod to accommodate itself to any position.

An important event in 1910 was the completion of the Ashendon-Aynho line, the last link in a shorter route between Paddington and Birmingham. Leaving the main line at Old Oak Common, the new route included the Great Western & Great Central Joint line from Northolt Junction to Ashendon through High Wycombe and Princess Risborough. It continued over the newly completed portion through Bicester to Aynho, where it joined the old line through Oxford, a little south of Banbury. This put the G.W.R. on an equal footing with the L.N.W.R. from Euston to Birmingham, and a service of trains was inaugurated to equal the timing of 2 hr. for the non-stop run of their competitors. In 1909, the Cunard Line decided to use Fishguard as a port of call, and special trains were run twice weekly in connection with the liners. In the following year the service was accelerated to do the journey to Paddington in 4 hr. 40 min. instead of 5 hr. The " Atbara " class were used between Fishguard and Cardiff, and the " Star " class onwards. Audible signalling, which had been in experimental use on the Fairford branch for some years, was installed between Paddington and Maidenhead. Superheating was extended to goods engines with plain slide valves, the 0-6-0 type " 2301 " class and the Armstrong goods.

The position of clackboxes had varied from time to time over the years. Whilst the side of the barrel, near the front end, had been the most usual place, clackboxes had been at other times on the back of the firebox, or even on the sides of the firebox. With the introduction of the domeless Belpaire boiler, the clacks were located on the bottom of the barrel, immediately behind the smokebox. The two boxes were side by side and attached to two branches of a " Y " casting bolted on the barrel and which carried a short hood inside to divert the incoming water from the vertical to the horizontal, so that it flowed along the barrel towards the firebox and was not discharged amongst the tubes, but promoted circulation of the boiler water in general. The difference in temperature between water in the boiler and that of the feed set up strains in the plate and this rendered it susceptible to corrosion by oxygen in the feed, originating from entrainment of air by the injectors and to air dissolved in the feed water, so that pitting was liable to occur along the bottom of the barrel. In some cases which I saw, the pitting and corrosion was particularly severe where the boiler was supported at mid-length on a frame stay so that mechanical as well as thermal conditions added to the strains locally.

All this was swept away when top feed was introduced in 1911. By this arrangement feed water was discharged on to trays in the steam space and trickled over into the boiler water, so that air was released into the steam space and precipitates from salts in the feed thrown down by the heating were dispersed over a wide area. Top feed had been tried in Germany in 1863 and in France in 1890, but had made no headway; in this new application at Swindon it was an undoubted success, due to the care taken initially. I well remember seeing trials being carried out adjacent to the drawing office, where the experimental tray was set upon a paved yard. A supply of metered water to represent the injector flow was brought to the discharge point by a hose and the water allowed to overflow on to the paving, whence it ran away to drain. The slope and shape of the tray was carefully adjusted until an even distribution was effected. When first fitted to domeless boilers, the clackboxes on top of the barrel had a separate seating in advance of the safety valve, but this was soon combined with the safety valve in a common seating. The separate seating was continued in the case of boilers having domes.

In 1910 it was explained to me that Churchward had completed his standard types for the main lines and that he was now turning his attention to secondary services. He did not wish to perpetuate the double-framed engines of the " Atbara," " Bulldog " and " Aberdare " classes which had many parts in common. What he had in mind was to replace them by a similar number of types but with inside frames, inside cylinders and 10 in. dia. long travel valves on top of the cylinders. I was instructed to prepare a scheme, but it did not take me long to discover many snags. It was one thing to have cylinders with slide valves or small diameter piston valves below them common to several types, as in the double-framed engines, but quite another to work in 10 in. piston valves above, due to encroachment on the smokebox.

Something might have been done with the small-wheeled 2-6-0 if single slide bars had been used to lessen the inclination of the cylinders necessary to clear the leading coupled axle, but Churchward would have none of it. He did not like the bulk of the crosshead being on one side of the cylinder centre line, as, with the least wear in it, the inertia of the mass at each end of the stroke would set up alternating stresses in the piston rod—crossheads must be symmetrical, he said. The " Kruger " had single slide bars and apparently he had some grounds for his objection as the result of experience. When he realised the impasse, Churchward went away to turn things over in his mind. He came up again a day or so later in conversation with the Chief Draughtsman and apparently he had been told of my observations on the use of the Mogul type, following my Canadian trip, for on reaching my board he said: " Very well then; get me out a 2-6-0 with 5 ft. 8 in. wheels, outside cylinders, the No. 4 boiler and bring in all the standard details you can." With that he departed, and it was the end of the matter as far as he was concerned.

It was as simple as that: this historic pronouncement was the means of setting up a milestone in the history of the locomotive in Great Britain, for it inaugurated the vogue of the general utility engine. Although no thought of it had entered into the decision, what had virtually been achieved was a tender engine edition of the " 3150 " class 2-6-2 tank. It was a matter of a few days to outline the new type, and, to reduce the length over buffers and overall wheelbase, I made use of the " Saint " class cab, which was the shortest, to secure the maximum of availability on lines where turntables might limit the use. As few drawings were required, material could be requisitioned straight away, and an order for 20 engines was placed on the shops.

The standard brake application valve and ejector with single cone which had served so well began to become inadequate with the ever-increasing train loads. New apparatus was therefore designed about 1911 in which the brake application handle merely governed the rate of air admitted to the train pipe. At the back of this valve, but quite independent of it, was the steam for operating the ejector, which was obtained from an internal supply pipe through a face joint on the firebox back. Two screw-down steam stop valves were embodied in this same casting. The ejector, which was fitted with a check valve, was placed outside the cab, a separate fitting located at the side of the firebox with an exhaust pipe carried to the smokebox by an external pipe alongside the boiler. This ejector had four cones, three of which were connected to one steam stop valve, and the fourth to the other valve. Thus either one, three or four cones could be used with one or other of the handles or by the use of both. Originally all four cones were supplied with steam from one connection. The use of separate steam to one cone came somewhat later. The single cone was intended for maintaining vacuum while the train was standing or in assisting the vacuum pump, if necessary, in running. Use of the three cones could raise vacuum quickly to release brakes, or all four cones could be so employed.

The general fitting of the four-cone ejector began about 1913. This type of brake application valve with separate handles saved a good deal of maintenance and a somewhat similar valve was designed for the smaller engines fitted with the vacuum brake, This had a face joint on the firebox back with an internal steam supply pipe for the single cone ejector at the back having an internal exhaust pipe to the smokebox; it included the check valve and drain. The separate steam valve was opened to release the brakes and the air valve to apply it. The large number of engines with steam brake continued to carry the original pattern of ejector with automatic valve for steam brake.

The first 2-6-0, No. 4301, made its appearance in 1911 and the others followed quickly. The running department was highly pleased to have a locomotive which they could put to so many uses, and was equally at home with passenger trains at 60 m.p.h. as with moderately heavy goods working. They found, however, that the injector gear was somewhat cramped. They would rather lose a little availability to have the trailing end lengthened to have more room for injectors. After the first 20, the engine was lengthened 9 in. at the footplate, a " County " class cab being used in place of the " Saint " class. With this one amendment, the type was built by the hundred in ensuing years, and other railways followed suit.

At this point I was told that Churchward was satisfied that he now had all the types necessary to operate the whole of the Great Western system, and that henceforth new construction would be to existing standard types. No new designs were likely to be undertaken in the drawing office for the next ten or fifteen years, except perhaps for one or two odd engines for special purposes, so that drawing office work would become routine and merely to keep the standards up-to-date by minor improvements as they came along from time to time.   There was no more new development work for me on the locomotive side and so they were transferring me to the general side of the office to tackle problems of a different and more varied nature.   So ended my participation in Great Western locomotive affairs; this remarkable experience was over before entering on my thirtieth year!

On the general side of the office, there was little that had any bearing on locomotive practice except perhaps the running sheds, of which I had experience in design of both the turntable and the straight types.   The general layout and details of construction were standardised, but the size of shed was adapted to the ground available and number of engines to be housed. The turntable type was preferred for the larger sheds.   These had 65 ft. tables with deep pit and inverted girders serving 28 pits per table.   Very little was required in the way of yard room for roads and sidings, and these sheds could often be accommodated on an odd piece of ground not suitable for the layout of a straight shed and its many outside roads.   The straight sheds were dead-ended and 180 ft. long.   Six roads per shed would house 18 tender engines and four-road sheds 12.   Where the small shed was remote from a large depot, a lifting shop with two roads was added for repair work. Turntables in the yard were often of the shallow pit type with girders above ground level.

All coal stages were of the elevated platform type with tip wagons, filled from coal wagons standing on an elevated road, being propelled there up a sharp gradient.   The G.W.R. did not favour mechanical coaling plants, as by the use of hand-filled tip wagons the issue of coal was much more selective and consistent.   The large lumps of first-grade Welsh coal could be reserved for the principal express locomotives and the rest used for less important duties.   Coal of a lower quality could be issued to goods engines and shunters.   In the Northern Division, the hard coals of North Wales and the Midlands were largely used, but in some cases a little Welsh coal for express work.

One scheme on which I was engaged in 1911 was for a droptable shop in the form of an annexe to the " A " erecting shop.   This was a building with a single road, long enough to take any locomotive and tender, present or prospective, and access was from off the turntable outside the erecting shop.   It contained a pair of short tables with pits, each 8 ft. long, which could be used individually or locked together as a unit to deal with complete bogies or the larger diameter driving wheels.   These lifts were hydraulically-operated from the mains and were powerful enough to take up the bearing spring loadings.   Behind and well clear of the locomotive and tender was a longer and lighter lift with flat top 16 ft. long, connected by a subway with the others, its purpose being to bring up a bogie or pair of wheels to the surface in rear of the locomotive so that they could be attended to or taken away to the main shops.

This annexe was intended primarily to deal with engines which developed heated bearings on trial trips. It would have obviated a good deal of dismantling and the uncoupling of the tender and have saved much time in dealing with scored journals or damaged axleboxes, and it would have reduced occupation of pit roads in the erecting shop and the use of the overhead cranes. An hydraulic capstan and reel were to be provided to haul the locomotive from turntable to drop pit and back. No doubt alternative uses would have been found for such a shop for other than trial engines, but the estimate of its cost of construction raised some doubt whether the expenditure would be justified, bearing in mind the case of the stationary testing plant, so the scheme was shelved.

On the locomotive side things turned out very much as anticipated; during the next ten years only two odd engines were designed, No. 4600, a 4-4-2 tank with 5 ft. 8 in. wheels and 17 in. by 24 in. cylinders appeared in 1913 and a large 2-8-0 mixed traffic engine with 5 ft. 8 in. wheels, No. 4700 in 1919. The tank engine was intended for passenger train working in Cornwall. Not being found so suitable as other types, it was stationed at Tyseley for suburban working, but it was not liked and therefore it was not repeated. The 2-8-0 represented an attempt to enlarge upon the " 4301 " class for extra heavy duties, by adding another pair of coupled wheels and substituting the No. 1 boiler for the No. 4; eight more of the 2-8-0 type, somewhat modified, followed later. Two years later the No. 1 boiler was replaced by a No. 7 boiler designed in 1920.

Standard types built between 1911 and 1922 included the last batches of " County " and " County " tank classes, more " Saints," " Stars," 2-8-0 and 2-8-0 tanks, 2-6-2 tanks. Above all, the " 4301 " class 2-6-0 was built by the hundred, more particularly during the 1914-18 war and in the immediate post-war years. Many of these 2-6-0 engines were shipped overseas to work on the military railways, where they gave excellent service. The last of the " County " class were put to work between Shrewsbury and Bristol.

Seen in retrospect, the Churchward era was in two parts. During the first decade came the creation of the standard types and the accomplishment of the task to which their designer had applied himself, so putting the Great Western some ten years or more ahead of other British railways and earning a reputation for himself which placed Churchward in the front rank of locomotive engineers of all time. Resting on his laurels, he was content to watch his standard types in action and others continuously rolling off the Swindon Plant to swell the numbers through the next decade, which ended in his retirement.

The Swansea District Railway was opened in 1914. It enabled Cunard specials from Fishguard and other trains to avoid the Cockett incline between Gowerton and Landore, consisting of 2¼ miles of 1 in 50 to 53 up, followed by 1¾ miles of 1 in 52 down, over which trains had to be banked. While piloting a passenger train one of Dean's double-framed saddle tanks of the " 1661 " class was derailed at high speed on the down gradient due to the fracture of a coupling rod, resulting in a serious accident at Loughor in 1904. From that time the use of such tanks on fast passenger trains was discontinued.

During the 1914-18 war, Swindon Works was much occupied in making munitions of war and new locomotives contruction was mainly concentrated on the " 4301 " class.   Control of the railways had passed to the Government through the Railway Executive Committee, and it seemed likely that the entire railway system of Great Britain would be taken over by the State after the war.   With a view to creating employment in the slump which would follow the war effort with the cessation of munition making, the Government wished to have some standard locomotive types on the drawing board, so that a large number of locomotives could be built to rehabilitate the railways as a whole, at the same time finding employment in the engineering industry.

The work of preparing the designs was entrusted to the A.R.L.E. other- wise the Association of Railway Locomotive Engineers.   This was a body composed of the heads of the locomotive, carriage and wagon departments of the United Kingdom and Ireland, who met periodically in pleasant surroundings at holiday resorts and incidentally to discuss matters in common. Being an existing body, they were brought together to produce standard locomotive designs which were the result of common agreement amongst the half-dozen or so more active members who participated.   Amongst these was Churchward, and much was due to his sage advice and wide experience that there was reconciliation of varying views expressed and sufficient harmony for designs to be well advanced for a 2-6-0 and a 2-8-0 type.   When Grouping of railways was decided on instead of State owner- ship, the four groups formed promptly rejected the standards created and proceeded to build to their own designs.   The Great Western was little affected by the change and missed the upheaval created elsewhere, and so carried on its own programme with the building of the " 4301 " class and the last batch of " Stars,"   Churchward retired at the end of 1921.

When R. E. L. Maunsell was appointed Chief Mechanical Engineer of the South Eastern & Chatham Railway, he drew heavily upon Swindon in 1914 in creating a new technical staff.   Seizing the opportunity of ultimately getting back on to locomotive work, I joined the little band of emigrants to found the first Great Western " colony."   It was not long before the Church- ward practices took root at Ashford, the coned Belpaire boiler, with top feed, the outside cylinders with 10 in. long travel valves and direct steam ports, the bush-end connecting rod, steel side stays for the firebox and many other details, found a place in new locomotive design.

After E. A. Watson had left Swindon to become C.M.E. of the Great Southern & Western, of Ireland, a four-cylinder 4-6-0 based on a set of drawings of the G.W.R. " Star"' class was built in 1921.   Inchicore drawing office failed to appreciate certain points in Churchward's design and the results of the engine in service were disappointing.   A few years later, Watson's successor sent a set of drawings of the Irish 4-6-0 to Waterloo, to see whether Maunsell, Watson's predecessor at Inchicore, could see any way of improving the engine.   The drawings were passed on to me for investiga- tion, but short of extensive rebuilding there was little that could be done. However, Churchward practices eventually found a place on Irish railways by devious paths when they purchased 2-6-0 type locomotives built at Wool- wich Arsenal to Maunsell's " N " class design.   These had coned Belpaire boilers, 10 in. long-travel piston valves, bush-type big-ends and other features of Swindon.

In 1932 another migration from Swindon took place on the appointment of W. A. Stanier (now Sir William) as Chief Mechanical Engineer of the London, Midland & Scottish Railway. This appointment ended the triangular contest between Derby, Crewe and Horwich by imposing Swindon practices on the lot!

Chapter Seven

ADVANCEMENT UNDER C. B. COLLETT

L OCOMOTIVE practice during Collett's tenure of office was no less successful than that under his predecessor. By adhering closely to the basic Churchward designs and enlarging them as necessary to meet ever-increasing demands by the Traffic Department, all such demands were covered by adequate motive power in a highly satisfactory manner.

One of Collett's first preoccupations in 1923 concerned the taking over of a number of Welsh railways and the Midland & South Western Junction Railway, which were brought into the Great Western sphere when grouping became effective. These included the Cambrian in Central Wales and the Taff Vale, Brecon & Merthyr, Neath & Brecon and other small lines in South Wales. The rolling stock had to be assessed as to general condition and some policy framed concerning future maintenance, particularly as regards boilers and the practicability of re-boiling when necessary by G.W.R. types to effect some standardisation and interchangeability. With the additional stock assimilated through grouping, the numbers were given as 1,486 tender engines and 2,415 tanks, a total of 3,910, plus 63 railcars.

Early in the new era, the bogie brake on express passenger engines came under review. Trials were made with and without the brake in operation, and it was established that the brake power exercised by the 13 in. cylinder made little or no difference to the distance run after full application of train brakes. It was therefore decided to strip off the bogie gear and so save shed maintenance on it; this had for long been an obvious thing to do, but no one dared to suggest it while the " Old Man " was in charge.

Construction of locomotives dating from orders issued under Churchward included ten of the " Star " class, the last batch to be made. These, the " Abbeys," Nos. 4063-73, had hollow crank axles. Other classes being turned out were 2-6-0 and 2-8-0 tender engines and 2-8-0 tanks. While private locomotive building firms had supplied a certain number of broad and standard gauge engines in the time of Gooch, the works at Swindon and Wolverhampton undertook all new construction under Armstrong and Dean. With the enlargement of Swindon Works in the early 1900s, this was concentrated on Swindon, and during Churchward's time the policy was continued, with the exception of the three French compounds and a number of Belpaire boilers furnished by contractors to expedite the re-boiling of the older engines with this type.

Under Collett, after the first few years, there was an increasing tendency to place orders for new construction on private firms, and many of the tank engines and some 2-6-0 tender engines were supplied by them. New design, which had virtually been at a standstill for 12 years, was resumed in 1923, when Collett planned a larger four-cylinder 4-6-0, the " Castle " class, parts. The cylinders were enlarged from the 15 in. diameter of the later " Stars " to 16 in., and a larger boiler, Standard No. 8, was installed. This was 3 in. more in diameter of barrel than the No. 1, and the firebox was lengthened to 10 ft., so increasing grate area from 27 to nearly 30 sq. ft. Maximum tractive effort was stepped up from 27,800 lb. to 31,625 lb. More generous provision for comfort was made in the cab, which had side windows and an extended roof.

The performance of the " Castle " class in service established Collett's reputation as a designer. It greatly enhanced the prestige of the G.W., and the General Manager's publicity officers saw to it that the attention of the travelling public was continually directed towards it through the issue of leaflets and booklets, such as " The Cornish Riviera Express" and "The 10.30 Limited." These centred round the running of the trains and descriptions of the " Castle " class, claimed to be " the most powerful passenger locomotive in Great Britain," based on nominal tractive effort! A number of through locomotive workings were instituted in 1924; these included Birmingham to Paignton, 202 miles, Paddington to Carmarthen, via Gloucester, 245 miles, and Paddington to Chester, 195 miles.

A break in the established G.W. practice occurred in 1924 by the building of the " 5600 " class 0-6-2 type tank. Various of the small railways in South Wales taken over on Grouping favoured this inside-cylinder tank engine, and the G.W. classes available in substitution did not fit in so well to their requirements, as the 0-6-2 tank was a very compact and handy type. Instead of allocating 2-6-2 outside-cylinder tanks and other classes to them, Collett wisely listened to the plea for the retention of the 0-6-2 tank and so designed a new engine at Swindon of this type, with 4 ft. 7½ in. wheels, using the standard No. 2 boiler, and incorporating all standard parts possible, such as pistons and valves. The wheels, hornblocks and valve gear were of new design, the valve gear being an adaption of that for the 18 in. by 30 in. outside cylinders to inside cylinders. A three-bar crosshead was adopted for the first time. In all, 200 were built in substitution for the older Welsh engines gradually withdrawn.

A new line was opened from Brettell Lane, near Stourbridge, to Oxley Sidings in 1925. It was a single-track extension of the double-track Kingswinford branch, and enabled South Wales coal trains and other through traffic to by-pass the congested section between Stourbridge Junction and Wolverhampton. Complementary to this was the provision of a large and well-equipped engine shed at Oxley, to which most of the freight engines from the old Stafford Road sheds were transferred. For a few years a steam railcar service was run over the line between Dunstall Park station, Wolverhampton, and Stourbridge Junction via Oxley, but this passenger service was eventually withdrawn.

Up to 1927, more " Castles " were being turned out, in company with 2-6-2 tanks of the " 4500 " series with 4 ft. 7½ in. wheels, the " 6300 " and " 7300 " series of 2-6-0 tender engines and more 2-8-0 tanks. There were also half-a-dozen small shunting tanks of the 0-4-0 type with cylinders and

Walschaerts valve gear outside the frames to give accessibility for oiling and
so avoid the necessity of doing so over a pit. These were of Avonside
Company design but to G.W.R. requirements as to certain details. They
were for use in sidings where very sharp curves existed. Churchward had
continued to build both " Stars " and " Saints " at intervals, but Collett
concentrated on the four-cylinder 4-6-0 and constructed no more " Saints."
In 1924 he took *Saint Martin* and rebuilt it with 6 ft. dia. wheels in place of
the original 6 ft. 8½ in. as an experiment. This produced important results
later.

In 1920 eight more of the " 4700 " class 2-8-0s with 5 ft. 8 in. wheels
had appeared, but, unlike the first, No. 4700, a new boiler, Standard No. 7*,
was installed with the same firebox and overall length as the " Castle "
boiler, No. 8, but larger in diameter in the barrel, 5 ft. 6 in. at front and 6 ft.
at back ring. The 19 in. by 30 in. outside cylinders had, as an innovation,
outside steam pipes from sides of smokebox direct to steam chests. The
engines were intended for hauling fast vacuum-fitted freight trains, such as
those between London and Bristol made up of 70 vehicles.

The "iron curtain" mentality that had previously resulted in the "splendid
isolation" of Swindon was greatly relaxed under Collett. The joint effort in
producing designs of standard locomotives by the A.R.L.E. had shown the
benefit of co-operation and the frank exchange of views. The 1920s and
1930s were times of mutual assistance between the Groups, tinged with
friendly rivalry.

By 1924 I was Technical Assistant on the S.R. Chief Mechanical Engineer's Personal Staff at the Waterloo Headquarters and in a position to know
most of what was going on. Here one would often see the imposing figures
of Collett or Gresley striding along the corridors, to or from a call on
Maunsell. Such visits were for exchange of views, discussion of knotty
problems and the framing of a common policy over some matter. Sir Henry
Fowler, a frequent visitor, was more affable and, after seeing the Chief,
would usually look in to " pass the time of day" with his assistants, next
door.

Every facility for mutual assistance was extended at all levels and placed
at the disposal of works managers, technical assistants, chief chemists and
foremen for visits to one another's shops to investigate practices and processes.
When there was difficulty in carrying out some special job, one works which
had the appliances would undertake to do it for another. My own experiences of such visits recall pleasant recollections of hospitality and courtesy
to a welcome guest, and of pains taken to give all information necessary and
to demonstrate anything in connection with the object sought. This was
particularly so where my former colleagues at Swindon were concerned.

To obtain a picture of the situation on the railways at the time, it is help-
ful to consider some external developments which reacted on Swindon

---

*Actually the Standard No. 7 boiler was designed under Churchward, who proposed fitting it to the
" Stars," " Saints," "2800" and " 4700 " classes. Diagrams showing the estimated weights were prepared in
May, 1919, but the Chief Civil Engineer vetoed the weights in the case of the " Stars " and " Saints " and
only the " 4700 " class received No. 7 boilers. Collett's No. 8 boiler is midway between Nos. 1 and 7

design, and to review the position of affairs on the other three Groups. The Bridge Stress Committee was set up in 1923 to investigate the stresses arising in underbridges by various loadings, spacing of wheels and hammer blows. Tests were carried out on selected bridges by running a number of differing locomotives from the several companies over various spans, and recorders were fixed to measure deflection of the bridges by the production of graphs over a range of speeds. The Chief Mechanical Engineer's representatives attended these trials as observers, and we saw, later on, some of the graphs produced by the recorders. It was notable that, owing to the lighter hammer blows, the graphs obtained from multi-cylinder engines lacked the deep serrations which indicated much higher peak loadings and a greater range of alternating stress set up by two-cylinder engines.

I had been for long an advocate of multi-cylindered locomotives and thought that their light hammer blows—or their total absence—merited some raising of the limit of the maximum permissible axle loading of coupled wheels; that is to say, axle load plus hammer blow should be taken together in the case of all locomotives, whether two-cylinder or multi-cylinder, and a combined maximum loading fixed. The light hammer blow should therefore permit more static axle loading within that limit. This point of view was pursued with the Civil Engineer's Assistants in informal discussion, and an examination of graphs and other records obtained by the S.R. bridge engineers of routine tests gave convincing evidence of the more favourable results from multi-cylinder engines. On reporting upon this to my immediate superior, he, in turn, put it to the C.M.E., who had some discussion with the Chief Civil Engineer on the subject.

The upshot of all this was a formal exchange of letters between them in which the C.M.E. enquired whether the C.C.E. would be prepared to accept axle loadings in excess of 20 tons in multi-cylinder engines and to what extent this increase could be. After referring the matter back to his Bridge and Permanent Way Assistants, the reply of the C.C.E. was that an increase up to 10 per cent. on the 20-ton loading would be favourably considered for full strength sections of the line.

At the grouping of the Southern Railway the Traffic Manager had set his requirements for the principal main line passenger trains as 500 tons tare weight, to be run at an average speed of 55 m.p.h. I had been engaged in outlining the motive power unit to cover this requirement, but with 20 tons as the maximum axleload it was evident that a 4-6-2 type would be needed to carry a boiler of adequate size. When the 10 per cent. concession in axle load was granted for multi-cylinder engines, it was possible with 22 tons as the limit to adopt the cheaper and simpler 4-6-0 type instead.

The proposal which I put up was for a four-cylinder 4-6-0 type engine with 17 in. by 26 in. cylinders and a boiler having, in round numbers, 1,900 sq. ft. of evaporative heating surface in tubes and 190 sq. ft. in firebox, 400 sq. ft. surface in superheater, with a grate area of 33 sq. ft. and a boiler pressure of 200 lb. per sq. in. With the standard S.R. wheel diameter of 6 ft. 7 in. it had a tractive effort of 14.03 tons and an adhesive weight estimated at 64 tons. The C.M.E., however, decided to raise the boiler pressure from the existing maximum of 200 lb. to 220 lb. per sq. in. and reduce the cylinders to 16½ in. in consequence, making the tractive effort 15.15 tons. He also decided to make use of alloy steel motion parts, so that with the weight saved thereby, the adhesive weight was reduced to 63 tons approximately.

With these amendments the outline diagram was submitted to the drawing office at Eastleigh for production of working drawings after going into the matter in detail, and in the summer of 1926 the prototype, No. 850, appeared and was named *Lord Nelson*. As it was some advance on the " Castle " in the matter of power, the S.R. General Manager's Publicity Department at once got to work to proclaim it as " the most powerful passenger locomotive in Great Britain," based, of course, on the tractive effort and so taking the wind out of the sails of the Paddington claimants!

In the spring of 1925 an exchange of locomotives took place between the L.N.E.R. and the G.W.R. A Gresley Pacific type, No. 1475, *Flying Fox*, was sent to the G.W.R. for trial and one of the G.W. " Castle " class, No. 4079, *Pendennis Castle,* to the L.N.E.R. As a result of experience gained, Gresley increased the travel of the valves of his 4-6-2 type by adopting a lap of 1⅝ in. and, later, raised boiler pressure from 180 lb. per sq. in. to 220 lb., with highly satisfactory results and an increase in power and efficiency. This was followed in the autumn of 1926 by the loan of " Castle " class engine No. 5000, *Launceston Castle*, to the L.M.S.R. for trial between Euston and Carlisle. This engine worked with ease the heavy services which were proving too much for the existing L.M.S. engines of 4-6-0 type, and so set a standard of performance to be emulated; and it could be anticipated that this might well come about in the near future.

On Grouping, the L.M.S.R. had adopted the Midland Railway system whereby a Superintendent of Operation, with a Superintendent of Motive Power under him, governed all rolling stock movements, so that the Running Department was divorced from the C.M.E. Department. Sir Henry Fowler's proposal to build a four-cylinder compound Pacific was unacceptable to the Motive Power Department, who objected to a 4-6-2 type, compounding, and the use of four cylinders if three would do the job; they could point out from experience that a 4-6-0 type comparable to the " Castle " was adequate.

Many locomotive engineers thought at that time that Southern locomotive practice was a jump ahead of the Great Western, as the principal features of Swindon design had been successfully adopted in conjunction with high superheat of 650F., and in some cases up to 700, so increasing the thermal efficiency of the steam cycle. Sir Henry Fowler was evidently of that opinion, notwithstanding the fine performance put up by the " Castle " on the L.M.S.R., for in his dilemma over the provision of adequate locomotive power to operate the projected Anglo-Scottish summer services of 1927, he turned to the Southern for assistance, sending his Chief Draughtsman to Waterloo to explain matters. As I was present at the interview, I can state the position broadly. Due to the delay arising from the rejection of the Pacific design, there was no time to build a prototype 4-6-0 and try it out in service; therefore, an existing design had to be taken as a basis, and the intention was to build a three-cylinder version of the S.R. *Lord Nelson*, using its boiler as the foundation and working in L.M.S.R. standard parts as developed at Derby for the wheels, framing and motion.

As a result of this appeal, a full set of S.R. drawings was sent to Glasgow and the whole of the resources of the North British Locomotive Co. Ltd. were devoted to the building of 50 locomotives as a rush job, delivery commencing in the summer. Early in March a preliminary drawing of the boiler was submitted to Waterloo for comment. Modifications included a shortening of the length of firebox by 3 in. and a corresponding lengthening of the barrel by that amount, to fit in with the general arrangement and the use of 6 ft. 9 in. coupled wheels. The barrel plates were slightly increased in thickness to permit raising boiler pressure from 220 to 250 lb. per sq. in.

It is therefore clear that the 15-year lead over the other railways which Churchward had established in 1911 had been swallowed up by 1926, locomotives of the other three Groups having overtaken it in power and efficiency. Thus, only four years after the " Castle " class had appeared, a further effort was called for if G.W.R. prestige was to be re-established. A Pacific type was not favoured, due to experience with *The Great Bear* and also arising from the results of the trial of the Gresley 4-6-2 on the G.W.R. in 1925.

The first indication that something was afoot at Swindon was the appearance of a " Castle " class engine with 6 ft. 6 in. coupled wheels in place of the standard 6 ft. 8½ in., late in 1926. Collett applied to the Chief Civil Engineer to ascertain whether the 20-ton maximum axleload could be exceeded, and he was informed that 22¼ tons would be accepted for four-cylinder locomotives on full-strength sections of the line. This opened the way to a heavier 4-6-0, as had been exemplified in the S.R. *Lord Nelson*.

The " Castle " class represented the extreme to which design could go while adhering strictly to the Churchward standards. A further enlargement of the basic four-cylinder design therefore necessitated a break-away from these standards. In the first place, 6 ft. 6 in. coupled wheels were adopted; new cylinders, enlarged to the extreme of 16¼ in. diameter and with the stroke increased from 26 to 28 in., had 9 in. dia. piston valves, a new size. The standard bar frame bogie with 3 ft. 2 in. wheels could not be used because of decreased clearances, and a new plate frame bogie with 3 ft. dia. wheels and with independent springing had to be designed; this was unique in having outside bearings to the leading pair of wheels and inside bearings to the trailing. The inhibition produced by the short life of the " Kruger " crank axles with their 14 in. throws had been forgotten in the generation which had elapsed, and so the new engine had a built-up crank axle with 14 in. throws. The motion arrangement originating with the " Star " class was, however, retained with little or no alteration. The boiler, Standard No. 12, a lengthened version of the No. 7 boiler, was 5 ft. 6 in. dia. on barrel, tapering to 6 ft. in a 16 ft. length, and the firebox was 11 ft. 6 in. long, with a grate area of 34.3 sq. ft. The working pressure was raised to 250 lb. per sq. in.

A very fine and handsome locomotive was the result, with a tractive effort of 40,300 lb. compared with 31,625 lb. of the " Castle," and an adhesive weight of 67 tons 10 cwt. as against 58 tons 17 cwt. Increase in maximum tractive effort was thus 27 per cent.; of this approximately $3\frac{1}{2}$ per cent. was due to larger cylinder bore, 8 per cent. to longer stroke, $3\frac{1}{2}$ per cent. from smaller wheel diameter and 12 per cent, to higher boiler pressure. Adhesive weight was increased by 15 per cent.

The names of kings of England carried by a batch of the " Star " class were transferred to the new engines, so that they became known as the " King " class. The ostensible reason for the construction of these locomotives was the ever-increasing train loads; yet it was but four years since the " Castle " was produced to cope with them, and therefore it might be said that they were in anticipation of even heavier loads. Not until 1930 were the platforms at Paddington extended to accommodate longer trains.

No. 6000, *King George V*, emerged at the end of July, 1927, a few weeks ahead of the L.M.S.R. *Royal Scot*, and so restored the prestige of the G.W.R. as regards locomotive power by an even bigger engine. It was shipped almost at once, with a reproduction of the *North Star*, to appear at the Centenary Celebrations of the Baltimore & Ohio Railroad in the early autumn of 1927. Afterwards it ran as an exhibit on several American railways before being returned to Cardiff Docks in November. The "King" class again featured strongly in publicity coming from Paddington, but the literature was more restrained and the fictitious claim of power based on maximum tractive effort alone, as in the case of the " Castle," was not repeated. In all, no more than 30 of the " King " class were constructed, as owing to the limited route availability they were confined to full-strength sections of the line, and distributed to work the heaviest trains between Paddington and Plymouth and Paddington to Wolverhampton via Bicester.

To undertake heavy repairs to locomotives in South Wales, important extensions were made to the former Rhymney Railway Works at Caerphilly and the works of the former Taff Vale Railway at Cardiff were closed, men and machines being transferred to these new Caerphilly shops in 1927. About this time the practice of providing deflector plates, on each side of the smokebox, began on the Southern and spread to other railways. The object of the plates was to deflect an air current to lift the smoke and exhaust steam clear of the cab windows on engines having large boilers and short chimneys. It is remarkable that such provision has not been found necessary on the Great Western.

Yet under certain atmospheric conditions, before the fitting of deflector plates, I had experienced total obscurity when riding on S.R. engines and the only way the driver could get a glimpse of the signals was to shut off steam momentarily at intervals, so losing time. That the trouble is much less on the G.W. and the plates not called for I attribute to four things: the smokebox is small in diameter because of the taper boiler and being flush with the boiler clothing plates; the chimney top stands higher from the smokebox due to this smaller diameter, while the corners of the Belpaire firebox cause eddy currents which tend to break up the stream of exhaust steam clinging to the boiler, before reaching the cab windows. Added to these is the audible cab signalling to give the driver confidence to keep going at full speed.

Following on the " Kings," construction during 1927-28 was devoted to the " 5500 " series of 2-6-2 tanks and to 0-6-2 tanks for South Wales. Some of the " 4300 " class of 2-6-0 tender engines were specially altered for use in Cornwall by modification to the pony truck, and renumbered as the 8300 series. The object was to carry more weight on the truck so that a greater side thrust could be safely taken by the flange through increased side control, thus relieving more pressure from the flange of the leading coupled wheels; tyre wear of coupled wheels on track abounding in curves was thereby reduced.

In 1928 came the first of the numerous " Hall " class, based on the rebuilt *Saint Martin* which had been given 6 ft. dia. wheels. No. 4901 was virtually Churchward's " Saint " class as regards boiler, cylinders, motion, frames and bogie, but with 6 ft. dia. wheels and the cylinder centre line coincident with the driving centre. It had a cab like that of the " Castle," with side windows and hand rail to roof. The type was intended as a general utility engine to replace not only the earlier of the " Saint " class, but also supersede the 4-4-0 classes with 6 ft. 8½ in. wheels, the " Atbaras," " Cities," " Counties" and " Flowers." All these had gone before 1934, as " Halls " were built.

More through engine workings were extended in 1928 by such runs as Banbury to Swansea via Cheltenham, 163 miles, and Birmingham, Swansea and Carmarthen, 195 miles. In 1929 came the first of the " 5700 " class of 0-6-0 pannier tanks, and their construction was continued steadily over the next 20 years, so that they became the most numerous of all classes. They were practically identical with the 2721 series of saddle tanks of 1897 as rebuilt with Belpaire boilers having domes and an enclosed cab. The wheels were 4 ft. 7½ in. and the slide valve cylinders 17½ in. by 24 in. There was no superheater, but pressure was raised from 180 to 200 lb. per sq. in. The first 50 came from the North British Locomotive Co. Ltd. These engines gradually replaced all the saddle tanks with 4 ft. 7½ in. wheels of the Armstrong and Dean designs built at Swindon and Wolverhampton. Some built in 1930 had side tanks and condensing apparatus and Weir feed pumps for service over the Metropolitan; these superseded the Wolverhampton side tanks of 0-6-0 type which had been adapted for this service.

Further 2-6-2 tanks with 5 ft. 8 in. wheels, the " 5101 " series, followed over 1929-30; these had outside steam pipes to the cylinders. In 1930 the building of 0-6-0 tender engines was resumed; more than 20 years had elapsed since the last of the " 2301 " class had been completed.

The " 2251 " class were replacements for the numerous Armstrong double-framed goods engines, and were intended for the lighter main line and branch freight services. They carried the No. 10 boiler, a domeless Belpaire with top feed; the 17½ in. by 24 in. cylinders, fitted with slide valves, were cast with the smokebox saddle. The wheels were 5 ft. 2 in. dia. and the motion was the same as the " 5700 " pannier tanks. The enginse had a steam brake and large cab with side window and handrails extended to roof. The No. 10 boiler was similar to Standard No. 3, but the length of firebox was reduced to 6 ft., giving a grate area of 17.4 sq. ft.

Over the period 1930-34 there was a remarkable revival of old designs of 50 or 60 years earlier, new engines being built to them after the basic design had been brought up-to-date. These were non-superheated engines with plain slide valves and a steam pressure of 165 lb. per sq. in. It was a case of the survival of the fittest where operation in service was concerned. In the first place one of George Armstrong's Wolverhampton shunting tanks of 0-6-0 type with 16½ in. by 24 in. cylinders, No. 2062, was rebuilt with 5 ft. 2 in. wheels in place of the original 4 ft. 1½ in. and pannier tanks substituted for the saddle tank. This was used for auto-train working and proved so successful that a batch of 20 new engines, the " 5400 " class, were constructed in 1930. This was followed by another batch of ten engines, the " 6400 " class, but these differed in having 4 ft. 7½ in. wheels; otherwise, boilers and other parts were the same. They were also fitted for auto-train working.

Next to be revived was George Armstrong's 0-4-2 tank, the famous Wolverhampton-built " 517 " class as modified with outside bearings to the trailing wheels. These economical little engines were non-superheater and with 16 in. by 24 in. cylinders and 5 ft. 2 in. coupled wheels. The pioneer, No. 1421, had been given a domeless Belpaire boiler and a weather-board fixed to the back of the bunker, and put into auto-train working at Cardiff in 1923.

Such working was extended by the building of new engines in 1932, modified to have 3-bar crossheads, as in the " 5600," " 5400 " and " 6400 " classes, and a drumhead smokebox carried in a saddle, screw reversing gear and an enclosed cab. This " 4800 " series (later re-numbered " 1400 ") was adapted for auto-train working, no fewer than 75 being built to supersede the older engines allocated to this duty as the steam rail motor cars were gradually withdrawn. The " 5800 " series of 20 engines of the same design followed, but these were not fitted for auto-train working. In 1924, six more of the " 1361 " class of outside cylinder 0-6-0 saddle tanks with Allan valve motion, with which I had been concerned in 1910, were completed, but this, the 1366 series had pannier tanks in place of the saddle type, and Belpaire fireboxes in place of round top. These small engines were indispensable in the docks and other places where the sidings were of sharp curvature. They replaced similar engines withdrawn through age.

In 1931 there was a speeding-up of fast-freight services at night, the average speed being raised to 40 m.p.h. One of these services was from Old Oak Common to Penzance, of which the 141½ miles from Newbury to Newton Abbot were non-stop. Another ran from Paddington to Birkenhead, being non-stop over the 145½ miles from Greenford to Shrewsbury. In the following year, a service was added from Paddington to Plymouth made up of 70 wagons; this also ran non-stop from Newbury to Newton Abbot. Automatic train control was completed from Paddington to Wolverhampton, to Swansea and to Plymouth. Apart from its safety aspect, this provision was of great assistance towards the maintenance of schedules during periods of fog.

By the beginning of 1932 new shops were made available at Stafford Road Works for handling the heaviest engines—the old Shrewsbury & Birmingham Railway shops could repair only the lighter engines. Through this modernisation it was no longer necessary to send other engines in the Northern Division to Swindon, which, like the Caerphilly shops in South

" Castle " class 4-6-0 No. 5010 *Restormel Castle* with 3,500 gal. tender. (141)

[*G. F. Heiron*

" Castle " class 4-6-0 No. 7000 *Viscount Portal* with 4,000 gal. tender. (159)

"King " class engine No. 6016 *King Edward V.* (145) with Driver Sam Bright and Fireman Ted Mitchel of Plymouth Laira Shed

[P. Ransome-Wallis
No. 4900, *Saint Martin* " Saint " class engine rebuilt with 6 ft. 0 in. coupled wheels. (142)

" Hall " class engine No. 4922, *Enville Hall*. (147)

" Modified Hall " class engine No. 6962, *Soughton Hall*. (158   [G. Wheeler

" Manor " Class engine No. 7810, *Draycott Manor.* (156) [*G. Wheeler*

" Grange " class engine No. 6828, *Trellech Grange.* (155) [*R. J. Buckley*

" County " class engine No. 1019, *County of Merioneth.* (158) [*G. Wheeler*

Left: "9400" class
0-6-0 Pannier Tank
No. 9400. (159)
[*G. Wheeler*

Centre: "1500" class
0-6-0 Pannier Tank
No. 1504. (160)
[*G. Wheeler*

Bottom: "1600" class
0-6-0 Pannier Tank
No. 1621. (160)
[*J. Davenport*

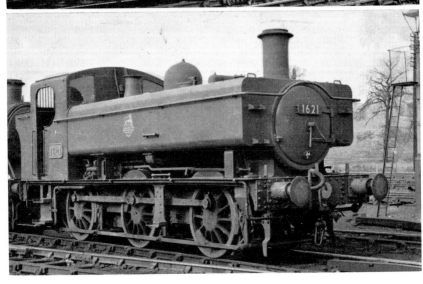

152

Wales, it relieved. The plan for the new shops at Wolverhampton was a revival in part of the scheme which I had been engaged on nearly 30 years before, and when it was shelved indefinitely.

In 1932 another migration of Swindon practices occurred when W. A. Stanier (now Sir William), Principal Assistant to Collett, was appointed Chief Mechanical Engineer of the L.M.S.R. Such influence was perhaps most marked in boiler design, and this successful application was, in course of time, carried over after Nationalisation into the design of boilers for the standard locomotives of British Railways. The first " Pacific " type of Stanier was virtually the G.W.R. " King " class extended to take a trailing truck, and a larger and longer boiler with wide firebox. The arrangement of cylinders and their dimensions, diameter and spacing of coupled wheels and boiler pressure were reproduced, so that the tractive effort was identical with that of the " Kings." It is remarkable that the low temperature super-heat which suited G.W.R. conditions, did not acclimatise itself to those of the L.M.S.R.; after experience with the first two engines, those following had the number of flue tubes in the boiler carrying superheater elements increased from 16 to 32, so doubling the superheater surface*. The equivalent of the " Hall " class was represented by the " Black Staniers," as the L.M.S.R. class " 5 " was dubbed.

The last of the 30 " Kings " had been completed in 1930, and it was significant that after a lapse of six years a resumption was made in 1932 of the building of the " Castle " class, and in all these totalled 171 in number eventually. Batches of these engines appeared from time to time over the next 18 years, alternating with further batches of the " Hall " class. This was parallel to the building of " Stars " and " Saints " in Churchward's day.

The numbers of the " Castle " class were augmented by conversion of 14 of the original " Star " class by rebuilding. The frames were lengthened by welding on new pieces in rear of the trailing wheels, the No. 8 boiler sub-stituted for the No. 1 and the improved cab was provided. Added to this rebuilding was that of No. 40, *North Star*, which had been converted from 4-4-2 to 4-6-0 type after a few years' running and renumbered 4000; and *The Great Bear*, No. 111, was converted from 4-6-2 to 4-6-0 type of " Castle " class and re-named *Viscount Churchill*, a total of 16 rebuilds. Commencing with No. 4093, the frame plates of the new " Castles " were 4 ft. 1 in. apart throughout their length, a pocket being pressed in at the front end to give clearance for the side movement of the leading bogie wheels. In the previous 20 engines and in the " Star " class, clearance had been obtained by reducing the width between frames to 3 ft. 5½ in. in advance of the outside cylinders by setting each inwards 3¾ in. with 6 in. radii in the form of a joggle. This, a source of weakness, was eliminated by the adoption of straight frames.

Because of the comparatively short distances between water troughs, tenders with a capacity of 3,500 gal. of water and six tons of coal sufficed for the " Star " class and other of the larger engines, even the special bogie tender for *The Great Bear* not exceeding this. There were a few 4,000 gal.

*With 16 elements it was found that the area through them was less than the area through the regulator valve and the steam pipes, and the steam inlet to cylinders was wire-drawn through them tenders of standard pattern in Churchward's day weighing 43 tons 3 cwt. when full, compared with 40 tons for the 3,500 gal. tenders, but the "Castle" class were at first provided with the normal 3,500 gal. tender.   Commencing with No. 5000, *Launceston Castle*, a new pattern of high-sided tender with a capacity of 4,000 gal. of water and six tons of coal was introduced, a development which enhanced the appearance of the locomotive.   It had an improved spring gear and the tank was simplified by having a flat bottom instead of being supplemented by a well between frames.   Hitherto the low-sided tender had been favoured on account of the facility it gave for coaling by hand methods through tip wagons on the high level coal stages.

About this time I came across one of my former Swindon colleagues who had become a responsible officer in the Running Dept.   In our conversation I remarked upon the fine performance set up by the " Castle " class engines with the " Cheltenham Flyer," timed to run the $77\frac{1}{4}$ miles from Swindon to Paddington in 65 minutes, and often done in less time. '' Actually,'' he said in confidential tone, '' it is one of our easiest jobs.'' '' Then why not run from Paddington to Swindon in 65 minutes?'' I asked, to which he replied, '' Ah, that would be a very different matter.''   My next query was: '' Could you not use the ' King ' class for it?'' and to this he remarked, '' As a matter of fact, the ' Castle ' is our best engine.''   He meant, no doubt that, as long as the job was within its capacity, they preferred to use a '' Castle '' rather than a '' King.''

About 1930 some development occurred to the triple sight feed lubricator of 1905.   The distributor box in the smokebox was abolished and the feed to each steam pipe was made direct through a spray nozzle projecting into the pipe.   The lubricator carried five glasses, two per steam pipe and one for regulator.   Each glass had independent adjustment under a master valve for overall control.   In a later development the lubricator had seven glasses in which two spare glasses were added, and the oil reservoir was in two compartments, that for cylinders holding 8 pints of oil and that for the regulator $1\frac{1}{2}$ pints.   Collett continued with compensating levers in the spring gear until about 1930, when, with the adoption of improved bearing springs, it was considered no longer necessary.

New methods of erection were brought into use about this time.   Jigs in the form of adjustable stands bolted to a bed plate in the floor were used for the assembly of frame plates and cross stretchers.   The frames were inverted, as this facilitated the setting of horns and the fitting of axleboxes in them.   When the assembly was complete, the framing was removed from the fixtures and turned over for transfer to the erection pit, where the cylinders were bolted on and set by optical means, in place of the former method by stretching twine or fine wire through them to the driving centre, to indicate the centre line.   The greater accuracy of the optical setting was reflected in the appreciably greater mileage of engines between general repairs.   The optical method was also used to set accurately the portable grinders used for re-facing horn surfaces during general repairs.

Jigs were set up for complete front end assembly.   The cylinders, extension frames, buffer beam and platforms were built up as a unit, complete with cylinder clothing and cocks.   Thus, the front end of an engine coming in for general repairs could be replaced by an interchangeable unit.   If necessary, bolting it to the main framing could be done without the removal of the boiler from its place.   Boilers, smokeboxes and ashpans were assembled in jigs, and then removed to a pit to receive a coating of magnesia insulation.   This was dried off by steam heating of the boiler, after which clothing plates, chimney, safety valve cover and all mountings were added so that the complete unit could be used for change of boiler when an engine came in for that purpose.   Such methods as these greatly reduced the time spent by an engine in shops.

In 1930 doubling of the line in Devon and Cornwall was completed, so that, with the exception of single line over Brunel's Saltash Bridge, there were 305 miles of double track between Paddington and Penzance.

One of the " Saint " class with $18\frac{1}{2}$ in. cylinders, No. 2935, *Caynham Court*, was fitted experimentally with a rotary cam poppet valve gear in 1931. It ran for some years, but no further engine was equipped.   On asking one of my Swindon friends about results from this gear, he told me that, while it gave more adequate opening for admission of steam, the opening to exhaust did not compare with that given by a large diameter long-travel piston valve; and there was no saving in fuel by its use.

The " Grange " class of 4-6-0 made its appearance in 1936: it was virtually the " Hall " class with 5 ft. 8 in. wheels in place of 6 ft.   It was, however, intended as an enlargement of the " 4301 " class 2-6-0, for there had for long been advocated in the Running Department the substitution of the No. 1 boiler for the No. 4, to give additional power and adhesion for some of the duties undertaken by these mixed-traffic engines, the last batch of which, the " 9300 " series, had been finished in 1932; these had outside steam pipes, screw reversers and the " Castle " type cab.   The " Grange " class were particularly useful for working perishable and seasonal traffic, such as fruit, broccoli and for excursion trains.   Usable parts taken from the older of the " 4301 " class engines withdrawn were absorbed in their construction.

Operation of traffic on the former Cambrian Railway presented a problem, for the conditions were not unlike those in Devon and Cornwall in 1895, where bridges and track were incapable of carrying engines of much weight, gradients and curves were severe, and there was a heavy holiday traffic to be contended with in the summer months over mainly single-line track.   This was characteristic of the Cambrian, with much seasonal traffic coming on to the system by way of Crewe or Shrewsbury to resorts on Cardigan Bay and elsewhere.

The " Duke of Cornwall " class had successfully operated in Devon and Cornwall from 1895, and so the class was re-constituted at Swindon in 1936 for the Cambrian by mounting " Duke " class boilers in the 4-4-0 type double-framed engines with 5 ft. 8 in. wheels still remaining in service, so extending their sphere of useful life in another field.   They were classified as new engines, numbered from 3200 onwards, and named after Earls;   29 were built in 1936-39.   Later, the names were removed and given to " Castle " class engines.   A prototype had been tried out in 1930 and numbered 3265, thus bringing the total to 30.

The change from coal to oil burning for boilers in the Navy and mercantile marine and the increasing number of diesel-driven vessels at sea had for many years brought about the gradual decline in the Welsh coal traffic to the docks.   As the 2-8-0 tanks of the " 4200 " class used in this work were becoming redundant, 50 of them were rebuilt at Swindon in 1934-36 as 2-8-2 tanks for main-line duties, by lengthening the frames at the trailing end and the addition of a radial truck, thus enabling coal and water capacities to be increased.   They were re-numbered from 7200 onwards; a further number were converted from 1937-39.   The 2-8-2 tanks were used to supersede the double-framed " Aberdares," which were then withdrawn.

In 1938 appeared the " Manor " class, a lighter 4-6-0, numbered from 7800 onwards.   This had 18 in. by 30 in. cylinders and 5 ft. 8 in. coupled wheels and a No. 14 boiler, a new standard with a coned barrel 4 ft. 7⅛ in. at front and 5 ft. 3 in. at back, with firebox 8 ft. 8⅝ in. long at top and 7 ft. 6 in. at foundation ring, giving a grate area of 22.1 sq ft.   A new departure was the set forward of the front water leg of the firebox.   The axle loading was little more than 17 tons, so enabling the class to operate on several hundred route miles from which the " Grange " class was barred.   They worked such turns as Banbury-Swansea with Newcastle-South Wales trains. They had outside steam pipes and the enlarged cab with side windows. Apart from the new boilers, cylinders and main frames, they were constructed by a system of cannibalisation, for " 4301 " class engines were withdrawn so that their motion and wheels were incorporated in the 4-6-0, the No. 4 boiler going into the pool of spare boilers, if still serviceable.   The " 8300 " series of the " 4301 " class, altered for service in Cornwall in 1928, were withdrawn, when their work was taken over by the new 4-6-0 classes, and they were altered back to conform to standard and re-numbered with their old numbers of the 5,300 series.

The intention of establishing a Locomotive Testing Station at Rugby, jointly by the L.M.S.R. and the L.N.E.R., led to a revival of interest in the Swindon plant by its modernisation in 1936 and the use of new techniques. It proved very useful in connection with boiler steaming trials and smokebox adjustments, but the realistic attitude at Swindon was always towards locomotive testing on the open road with suitable train loads of normal stock and the intervention of the dynamometer car.   By further additions to the apparatus of the car and the development of what was known as the Controlled Road Testing System, linking the thermo-dynamics of the locomotive with the mechanics of the train, an assessment could be made of the efficiency and capacity of the locomotive within its economic range.

Between 1937 and 1940, ten of the later " Star " class, the " Abbeys," were rebuilt as " Castle " class, Nos. 5083-92.   Early in 1939, two new varieties of 2-6-2 tanks appeared.   The " 8100 " class of ten engines* were similar to the " 6100 " class of 1931 carrying a No. 2 boiler pressed to 225 lb. per sq. in., but the coupled wheels were of a new size, 5 ft. 6 in. in place of 5 ft. 8 in. in order to improve the acceleration of suburban passenger trains and the pony truck wheels 3 ft. in diameter instead of 3 ft. 2 in.   The cylinders remained 18 in. by 30 in., so that the smaller wheels raised tractive effort from 27,340 lb. to 28,165 lb.

---

*The ten engines of the " 8100 " class were obtained by converting some of the old " 3100 " class of 1903-1906.

A new 3100 class*, carrying t e numbers of Churchward's original 2-6-2 tanks, had a No. 4 boiler pre d to 225 lb. per sq. in. and 18½ in. by 30 in. cylinders, but the coal carried was 3¼ tons instead of 4 tons. The coupled wheels were of a new size, 5 ft. 3 in., and the pony truck wheels 3 ft. Tractive effort was thus raised to 31,170 lb. As these engines are used for banking, the coupled wheels were reduced in size as maximum boiler demand is not sustained and maximum speed is comparatively low. The break-away from the Churchward set of wheel diameters, which began with the "King" class, led to the creation of 6 ft. 6 in., 6 ft., 5 ft. 6 in. and 5 ft. 3 in. dia., while the new 3 ft. size of bogie wheel was adopted for the pony trucks of these tank engines.

Up to the outbreak of the second world war in 1939, apart from the various 4-6-0 types, " Castles," " Halls," " Granges " and " Manors," new construction in the preceding five years had included numerous 2-6-2 tanks with 5 ft. 8 in. wheels, more of the 0-6-0 light goods and some 2-8-0 mineral engines. Above all, the pannier tanks of several designs were built in quantity, most of them being of the " 5700 " class. Others included the " 5400 " and " 6400 " class fitted for push-and-pull trains and 30 of the " 7400 " class of the same design not so fitted, but with boiler pressure raised to 180 lb. per sq. in., so increasing their tractive effort.

Under war conditions, the Railway Executive Committee assumed overall control and several orders for new engines were cancelled; old engines withdrawn from service were brought in, given a general repair and put back into traffic. New construction was confined to general utility engines, the " Hall " class and 2-6-2 tanks, and freight engines of 2-8-0 and 0-6-0 types.

In the summer of 1941 Collett retired.

---

*The five engines of the new " 3100 " class were conversions of the " 3150 " class of 1906-1908

Chapter Eight

FINALE UNDER F. W. HAWKSWORTH

UNLIKE his predecessors in office, who had received their early training elsewhere, F. W. Hawksworth was born at Swindon and had spent the whole of his career on the Great Western. Under Churchward and Collett he had progressed from time to time until he became Principal Assistant to the C.M.E. On Collett's retirement, Hawksworth was appointed Chief Mechanical Engineer in July, 1941. Under war conditions with Government control exercised through the R.E.C., there was not much scope for development, and it was mainly a question of carrying on with the orders on hand when he took over. Beyond this, the shops were occupied in building 80 engines of 2-8-0 type, class " 8F " of L.M.S.R. design.

In 1944 he made some important modifications to the " Hall " class, commencing with No. 6959. The arrangement with cylinders bolted back to back with smokebox saddle in combination with bar extension frames, originating in Churchward's No. 98, was abandoned in favour of individual castings bolted to the outside of the main frames, which were extended to the front buffer beam. A fabricated structure with smokebox saddle formed the stay between cylinders. The bar frame bogie was superseded by one of plate framing with individual springs and with wheels 3 ft. in diameter, as in the " King " class. The No. 1 boiler was modified by having the superheater surface increased from 262.6 sq. ft. to 314.6. This was the result of adopting 21 flue tubes in place of 14, reducing the small tubes from 176 to 145 in number, thereby altering the evaporative surface of the boiler from 1841.3 to 1737.5 sq. ft. These alterations resulted in an increase in weight of engine by 16 cwt. Altogether 71 engines were made to this pattern.

With the ending of the war in 1945, Hawksworth produced his " County " class of 4-6-0 type. This was a two-cylinder design and virtually an enlargement of his modified " Hall " class, but the coupled wheels were increased to 6 ft. 3 in. in diameter, yet one more departure, the sixth, from the Churchward standard wheel sizes. The cylinder dimensions and type of bogie were the same as in the modified " Hall," as also the wheelbase. A new boiler, Standard No. 15, was 5 ft. dia. at front ring and 5 ft. $8\frac{3}{4}$ in. at back; the firebox was 9 ft. 9 in. at top and 9 ft. 3 in. long, at foundation ring, giving a grate area of 28.8 sq. ft., the front water leg being set forward as in the No. 14 boiler. The working pressure was increased to 280 lb. per sq. in. The chimney fitted to the first engine, No. 1000, was a double one, the blast pipe being duplicated, but engines built subsequently reverted to the normal type of chimney. The 4,000-gal. tender was of a new design with flat sides and deep frame plates with large holes slotted out between wheels. The coal capacity was increased to 7 tons. These modifications added 2 tons 6 cwt. to bring the total weight in working order to 49 tons.

Owing to the weight carried on the coupled wheels, 19 tons 14 cwt. per axle, and the heavier hammer blow resulting from the use of two cylinders, the " County " class was permitted to run only on routes available to the " King " class at unrestricted speed.   Elsewhere it was subject to restriction in maximum permissible speed.   In total weight and tractive effort, the " County " was practically the same as the " Castle," though, being a two-cylinder, it was cheaper to produce.   A close resemblance in outline and dimensions and in heating surfaces is to be noted between the No. 15 boiler and that of the L.M.S.R. class " 8F ", built in quantity in Swindon Works during the war.   Actually the flanging blocks for the " 8F " boiler were used for the No. 15 boiler.

As well as the " Counties," new construction after the war included " Castles," " Halls," and " Manors," as also several classes of pannier tank engines.   The modification of the No. 1 boiler for the " Hall " class by the adoption of three rows of flue tubes in place of two, in order to carry more superheater elements to increased superheat, was extended to the No. 8 boiler for the " Castles," commencing with No. 5098 in 1946.   The " 7000 " series which followed also had more superheat and they were provided with the flat-sided tenders introduced with the " Counties."

A still higher degree of superheat was provided on No. 5049 in 1947, when it received a boiler with four rows of flue tubes in which the elements had a total of 393 sq. ft. of surface.   The sight feed lubricator gave way to a mechanical lubricator to feed cylinders, valves and regulator, as a matter of expediency.   In the early days of superheating, trials had shown the sight feed lubricator to give better results than the mechanical with the low degree of superheat, hitherto prevailing.   My experience on the Southern with both types of lubrication in use on the same class of engine with high superheat was that the sight feed gave rather the better results as regards efficiency of lubrication and there was less carbonisation in valves and cylinders.   It was cheaper in first cost and in maintenance.   The mechanical lubricator is, however, more suited to present-day conditions of running where pooling of engines is in force.   It needs replenishing less often and saves preparation time, as it is looked after by shed staff.

The General Election in the autumn of 1945 brought into power a Socialist Government whose policy promised State ownership of industry, and a plan for the unification of the four railway groups under Nationalisa-tion was one of their first tasks.   The imminence of this created a situation in which any thoughts of further development were discouraged.   While no major new design was attempted, Hawksworth did, however, create three new classes of pannier tanks.   The first to appear was the " 9400 " class of 1947, a modification of the " 8750 " class and suitable for either shunting or local passenger work.   This had inside cylinders with slide valves, 17½ in. by 24 in., as used in the " 2251 " class goods, and 4 ft. 7½ in. wheels.   It carried the coned and domeless boiler No. 10 in a saddle; this was pressed to 200 lb. per sq. in. and had a grate area of 17.4 sq. ft., a superheater* with 74 sq. ft. surface and top feed.   A cab wider than normal was provided; motion was common with that of the " 2251," " 5700 " and " 8750 " classes.

*The superheaters were subsequently removed: only the first 10 engines carried them.

The earlier " 8750 " class had a " 2301 " class boiler, parallel barrel and with dome. The next design, the " 1500 " class, was of the same leading dimensions as the " 9400 " class, but the No. 10 boiler carried was without superheat. It had outside cylinders with 8 in. piston valves driven by Walschaerts gear, the object being to give facilities for oiling from the ground, an advantage in busy shunting yards for which the class was intended. The wheelbase was short, only 12 ft. 10 in., so that sharp curves of 3 ch. radius could be taken at slow speed, but the large overhang resulting at each end made the engine unsuitable for running at any but very moderate speed. It had the wide cab also, and the tanks carried no less than 1,350 gal. of water and the bunker 3 tons 6 cwt. of coal, so that the total weight in working order was higher than normal, being 58 tons 4 cwt.

Lastly, there was the " 1600 " class pannier tank, a modernised version of the " 2021 " class Wolverhampton saddle tanks for shunting duties dating back over 70 years, which it replaced. This had $16\frac{1}{2}$ in. by 24 in. inside cylinders with slide valves and Stephenson gear, and 4 ft. $1\frac{1}{2}$ in. wheels. The No. 16 boiler had nickel steel plates and was parallel and with dome, the diameter of barrel was 3 ft. 9 in. and the firebox 5 ft. long. The pressure was 165 lb. per sq. in.

On December 31, 1947, the Great Western Railway Company came to an end and on the following day the system became known as the Western Region of British Railways, responsibility for design, repairs and running passing to the control of a Central Office of the British Transport Commission. At this period there were many uncompleted orders on the Works for new locomotives and others on which no start had been made. Higher super-heat was being tried on the " King " class, by increasing the number of flue tubes from 16 to 32 in number. There was thus a period of transition, and Hawksworth remained on for two years to see the bulk of these through shops before he retired from railway work, the task for which he was destined unfulfilled. In the brief period in which he was able to show his hand, he departed from the frame and cylinder arrangement of Churchward in the modified " Halls " and the " Counties." On these " Halls " and the later built " Castles " there was a cautious approach to the use of a higher degree of superheat. The experience of Stanier on the L.M.S.R. with his first Pacifics threw doubts on whether the Great Western was pursuing the right policy by adhering to the low superheat which satisfied Churchward and Collett.

For 110 years Great Western locomotive practice, alone of all English railways, had been carried through by an unbroken succession of men steeped in the traditions of a famous company. It passed from one to another as a smooth, continuous development, each one making his own contribution to the process and handing it on to the next. Design, construction, running and maintenance were intimately associated and they remained under one head throughout.

Chapter Nine

EPILOGUE

THE advent of nationalisation in 1948 brought to an end Swindon's long reign as the *fons et origo* of celebrated locomotives of distinctive design. For some years, however, the construction programme of existing classes was allowed to continue as planned, particularly with such types as 0-6-0 tank engines where British Railways standard designs were not as yet contemplated.

The building of " Castles " and " Halls " continued until the end of 1950, after which ten more of the " Manor " class brought the construction of tender engines of Great Western design to an end. Swindon Works then turned to the construction of British Railways standard types, in which a number of Great Western features are noticeable, particularly in the boilers.

Early in 1948 an order for 150 pannier tanks of the " 94XX " class, having 4 ft. 7½ in. wheels, was placed with contractors; it was distributed between several firms and has been spread over about seven years. Swindon Works took up again the building of pannier tanks of the " 16XX " class with 4 ft. 1½ in. wheels in 1950-51, notwithstanding the large number of diesel-electric shunters being built elsewhere.

With Hawksworth's retirement at the end of 1949, the works, running and carriage and wagon departments, which had, in accordance with Great Western traditions, all come under the Chief Mechanical Engineer, were separated.

Recent events have brought the end of steam locomotive construction for British Railways into closer view; so perhaps in any case the Swindon story was almost complete in this respect and Churchward's vision had become a solid achievement. As on many railways projected designs were got out from time to time, but never passed beyond the Drawing Office. In general it may be said that most of these would have had but very limited use where not already catered for by an existing class and unneccesary multiplication of types was not likely to find favour with the very realistic management of the old G.W.R.

Not only in design has Swindon been noted, but also for its very practical approach to locomotive testing, having introduced the first dynamometer car in the world and the first stationary test plant in Great Britain. In this respect most important work has been continued since 1948 in perfecting techniques to produce results of unprecedented exactitude.

The principal object of testing has been to ascertain the thermo-dynamic performance of the engine and to relate this to the mechanics of hauling trains. With many variables this is not an easy matter. Most of such testing in the past has been done on the basis of constant speed, which

161

presents practical difficulties. Swindon, however, has been developing a very successful alternative method based on constant steam rates. By means of a simply devised steam-flow meter it has been found unexpectedly easy for the engineman to maintain the desired conditions at various rates of output. The driver manipulates regulator and cut off in accordance with a fixed point on the flow meter in the cab. The fireman, having built up a uniform fire of the depth best suited to the type of coal, fires at a more or less uniform rate varied only when indicated by the pressure gauge. Under these conditions the water level in the boiler can be kept to within $\pm \frac{1}{8}$ in. Furthermore, this procedure is very similar to the manner in which many engine crews tend to work naturally.

With this Controlled Road Testing System it is possible to predict very exactly and much more precisely than previously the performance of a locomotive at a selected rate of steam flow over various routes and with different loads. Hence the preparation of timetables and new workings is greatly simplified. One of these tests shows No. 6001 *King Edward VII*, then 26 years old, hauling a 796-ton train on a fast schedule at a steam rate of 30,000 lb./hr.—an achievement far greater perhaps than the introduction of a new and more powerful design of express passenger locomotive. These developments have been under the direction of S. O. Ell, who read a most interesting paper on the subject before the Institution of Locomotive Engineers in 1953. Amongst the many interesting points brought out was the vexed question of driving on the regulator versus cut-off. Below $17\frac{1}{2}$ per cent cut-off it is more economical to work on the regulator, but above this full regulator and variable cut-off has the advantage, though not very great. Also that the grate limit is attainable with narrow fireboxes but not with the wide type.

From the point of view of locomotive design these tests have led to closer investigation of the smokebox, the importance of which has often been underestimated in the past. Efficient draughting and lifting of the smokebox gases is best achieved when the velocity at the nozzle of the blastpipe is not too high. This has a better lifting effect on the gases, avoiding the tendency of the jet to " cut through " them and the uncontrolled expansion of the steam at its periphery. We now see " Kings " with double chimneys and other modifications both on former G.W.R. and other regional types resulting in improved performances of 25 per cent. to 100 per cent. This in itself is a great achievement and one wonders what might have been done on these lines with some now defunct bad steamers of the past.

Great Western influence can also be seen in other ways, notably in the introduction of precision methods into locomotive shops in this country. Much work has been done on this by K. J. Cook, who succeeded F. W. Hawksworth as Mechanical and Electrical Engineer of the Western Region before taking up his present position as Chief Mechanical and Electrical Engineer, Eastern and North Eastern Regions, at Doncaster. The first optical frame and horn lining up apparatus was installed at Swindon in the early 1930s. This was followed by most accurate methods of gauging such fundamental dimensions as crank pin angle and throw. Great precision in engines turned out from shops has been more than repaid by increased mileages between general overhauls, for which the G.W.R. was noted.

As to future forms of motive power, one of the contestants and perhaps one of the most promising is the gas-turbine-electric locomotive.   The introduction of this new type of prime mover into Great Britain was instigated under Hawksworth at Swindon One unit was obtained from Brown-Boveri, Switzerland, and this was followed by another of an alternative design from Metropolitan-Vickers, Manchester. For entirely novel prototypes they have achieved some remarkable performances and a large mileage. Results in service have been encouraging, and the recent advances in gas-turbine design suggest that even better results are attainable.